REGENTS RESTORATION DRAMA SERIES

General Editor: John Loftis

OROONOKO

THOMAS SOUTHERNE

Oroonoko

Edited by
MAXIMILLIAN E. NOVAK
and
DAVID STUART RODES

UNIVERSITY OF NEBRASKA PRESS
LINCOLN

Publishers on the Plains

Thanks are due to Random House, Inc., for permission to quote
from W. H. Auden, "Musée des Beaux Arts," in *Collected Shorter
Poems, 1927–1957* (New York, 1967).

Library of Congress Cataloging in Publication Data

Southerne, Thomas, 1660–1746.

Oroonoko.

(Regents restoration drama series)

Present text based on 1st ed. printed for H. Playford, B. Tooke, and
S. Buckley, London in Dec. 1695, with 1696 t.p. date.

Includes bibliographical references.

1. Slavery in Surinam—Drama. I. Novak, Maximillian E. II. Rodes,
David Stuart. III. Title.

PR3699.S306   1976   822'.5   75–38054

ISBN 0-8032-9292-9

Regents Restoration Drama Series

The Regents Restoration Drama Series provides soundly edited texts, in modern spelling, of the more significant plays of the late seventeenth and early eighteenth centuries. The word "Restoration" is here used ambiguously and must be explained. A strict definition of the word would be unacceptable to everyone, for it would exclude, among many other plays, those of Congreve. If to the historian it refers to the period between 1660 and 1685 (or 1688), it has long been used by the student of drama in default of a more precise term to refer to plays belonging to the dramatic tradition established in the 1660s, weakening after 1700, and displaced in the 1730s. It is in this extended sense—imprecise though justified by academic custom—that the word is used in this series, which includes plays first produced between 1660 and 1737. Although these limiting dates are determined by political events, the return of Charles II (and the removal of prohibitions against operation of theaters) and the passage of Walpole's Stage Licensing Act, they enclose a period of dramatic history having a coherence of its own in the establishment, development, and disintegration of a tradition.

The editors have planned the series with attention to the projected dimensions of the completed whole, a representative collection of Restoration drama providing a record of artistic achievement and providing also a record of the deepest concerns of three generations of Englishmen. And thus it contains deservedly famous plays—*The Country Wife*, *The Man of Mode*, and *The Way of the World*—and also significant but little known plays, *The Virtuoso*, for example, and *City Politiques*, the former a satirical review of scientific investigation in the early years of the Royal Society, the latter an equally satiric review of politics at the time of the Popish Plot. If the volumes of famous plays finally achieve the larger circulation, the other volumes may have the greater utility, in making available texts otherwise difficult of access with the editorial apparatus needed to make them intelligible.

The editors have had the instructive example of the parallel and senior project, the Regents Renaissance Drama Series; they have in fact used the editorial policies developed for the earlier plays as their own, modifying them as appropriate for the later period and as the experience of successive editions suggested. The introductions to the separate Restoration plays differ considerably in their nature. Although a uniform body of relevant information is presented in each of them, no attempt has been made to impose a pattern of interpretation. Emphasis in the introductions has necessarily varied with the nature of the plays and inevitably—we think desirably—with the special interests and aptitudes of the different editors.

Each text in the series is based on a fresh collation of the seventeenth- and eighteenth-century editions that might be presumed to have authority. The textual notes, which appear above the rule at the bottom of each page, record all substantive departures from the edition used as the copy-text. Variant substantive readings among contemporary editions are listed there as well. Editions later than the eighteenth century are referred to in the textual notes only when an emendation originating in some one of them is received into the text. Variants of accidentals (spelling, punctuation, capitalization) are not recorded in the notes. Contracted form of characters' names are silently expanded in speech prefixes and stage directions, and, in the case of speech prefixes, are regularized. Additions to the stage directions of the copy-text are enclosed in brackets.

Spelling has been modernized along consciously conservative lines, but within the limits of a modernized text the linguistic quality of the original has been carefully preserved. Contracted preterites have regularly been expanded. Punctuation has been brought into accord with modern practices. The objective has been to achieve a balance between the pointing of the old editions and a system of punctuation which, without overloading the text with exclamation marks, semicolons, and dashes, will make the often loosely flowing verse and prose of the original syntactically intelligible to the modern reader. Dashes are regularly used only to indicate interrupted speeches, or shifts of address within a single speech.

Explanatory notes, chiefly concerned with glossing obsolete

words and phrases, are printed below the textual notes at the bottom of each page. References to stage directions in the notes follow the admirable system of the Revels editions, whereby stage directions are keyed, decimally, to the line of the text before or after which they occur. Thus, a note on 0.2 has reference to the second line of the stage direction at the beginning of the scene in question. A note on 115.1 has reference to the first line of the stage direction following line 115 of the text of the relevant scene. Speech prefixes, and any stage directions attached to them, are keyed to the first line of accompanying dialogue.

JOHN LOFTIS

Stanford University

Contents

List of Abbreviations

Behn	*Oroonoko; Or The Royal Slave*. In *The Works of Aphra Behn*, ed. Montague Summers, 5 vols. London, 1915; reissued New York, 1967. 5: 125–208.
C1	Collected works, duodecimo, 1713
C2	Collected works, duodecimo, 1721
DNB	*Dictionary of National Biography*
H	An edition printed in The Hague, octavo, 1712
OED	*New [Oxford] English Dictionary*
om.	omitted
Q1	First edition, quarto, 1696 [1695]
Q2	"Second Edition," quarto, 1699
Q3	Another edition, quarto, 1699
S	An edition, sexto, 1736
S.D.	stage direction
S.P.	speech prefix
Tilley	Morris Palmer Tilley. *A Dictionary of Proverbs in the Sixteenth and Seventeenth Centuries*. Ann Arbor, 1950.

Introduction

The present text of Thomas Southerne's *Oroonoko* is based
principally on the first edition, a quarto (Q1) published in
December 1695, probably within a month of the first performance.
The title page bears the date 1696, and the edition was printed
for H. Playford, B. Tooke, and S. Buckley.[1] There is no entry
for the edition in either the Stationers' Register or the Term
Catalogues,[2] but *Oroonoko* was advertised for sale in both the
Post Boy, 12–14 December 1695, and the *London Gazette*, 12–16
December 1695. The notice in the *London Gazette* seems to
establish the exact date of publication as Monday, 16 December
1695: "This day is Published Oroonoko, a Tragedy, as it is Acted
at the Theatre Royal by His Majesties Servants. Writted by Tho.
Southerne."

In 1699, two more quarto editions appeared, both set, inde-
pendently, from Q1. One of these (Q2) is called "The Second
Edition" on its title page and was printed for H. Playford and
B. Tooke.[3] The other 1699 edition (Q3) has title pages in two
different states, one printed for Playford, Tooke, and "*A. Bettesworth*," with a list of "Newly Published" books at the bottom of
the page,[4] and the other printed for Playford, Tooke, and "*R.
Bettesworth*," with a different list of works advertised on the

1. Q1 is described bibliographically as follows: [A1r]-[M3v] in fours;
[viii], 1–84, [2]. Wing S–4761. Copies collated: William Andrews Clark
Memorial Library (CLC), *PR3699/S307; Henry E. Huntington Library (CH), 64330; and Folger Shakespeare Library (F), S4761.
2. The Term Catalogue for Michelmas Term, 1695, in which one
would expect to find the announcement of the play, is not extant.
3. Q2 is described: [A1r]-[H4v] in fours; [vi], 1–58; Epilogue immediately follows Prologue. Wing S–4763. Copy collated: CLC, *PR3699/
S307/1699c.
4. Copy collated: Q3 (CLC, *PR3699/S307/1699a); Wing S–4764;
Woodward and McManaway call this (1168) "another issue of the 1st
1699 ed." Q3 (CLC) is described: [A1r]-[L3v] in fours; [viii], 1–[78];
[L4], which presumably contained the Epilogue, is omitted; pages
15 and 78 misnumbered 14 and 80, respectively, as in Q3 (F).

title page and with additional lists on the versos of the title page and Epilogue.[5] There are no other important substantive variants between these two states of Q3. Of the two 1699 quartos, Q2 is printed less exactly, its text crowded into fewer pages; Q3 follows and often corrects printing errors in Q1. These three quartos are the only seventeenth-century editions of the play.

We have collated four eighteenth-century editions. The earliest of these is an octavo (H) printed in 1712 "for T. JOHN-SON./Bookseller at the Hague;"[6] it was set from Q3. Another edition, a duodecimo (C1),[7] is included in the first collected edition of Southerne's plays, *The Works of Mr. Thomas Southerne* (London, 1713), 2: [177]–[266].[8] Though this *Oroonoko* was also set from Q3, it may be the only text except Q1 which has separate authority. In his Preface to the *Works*, Southerne claims: "I Have done my Part in this Edition of my Plays, by carefully examining the several Copies, and correcting the many Errors

5. Copy collated: Q3 (F, S4762/ca368); Wing S–4762; Woodward and McManaway 1169. Q3 (F) is described: [A1r]–[L4v] in fours; [viii], 1–[78], [2]; page 47, number missing. This copy adds a list of books printed for R. Wellington [A1v] and lists of books for B. Took[e] and for R. Wellington [L4v]. [L4r] contains the Epilogue.

6. H is described: [A1r]–[G6v] in eights; [x], [11]–108; page 40 misnumbered 38; page 105 misnumbered 104. Copy collated: CH, 11999.

We have collated another edition of *Oroonoko* which is related closely to this pirated Hague edition of Thomas Johnson. It is included in Volume V of *A Collection of the Best English Plays*, a series of plays published in Holland which are extant as collections in three different states issued in 1711–18, 1720–22, and 1750. We have collated a copy of the second issue (British Museum: 1345.G.20), but have not included its readings in the Textual Notes since there are no significant variants from H and since it can have no textual authority. The best published information on Thomas Johnson and on this collection is in H. L. Ford, *Shakespeare 1700–1740* (Oxford, 1935), pp. 46–52.

7. C1 is described: [H5r]–M1v in twelves. Copies collated: CH, 125195 (Hoe); CH, 125194.

8. There are two variant states of the general title page: one printed for Jacob Tonson and Benjamin Tooke (CH, 125194 [Hoe]); and another which adds the imprint of Bernard Lintott (CH, 125194). The individual title page is the same in both copies: "*OROONOKO*./ A/ TRAGEDY./ As it was Acted at the/ THEATRE ROYAL, . . . In the Year 1699 . . . . Printed in the Year 1713."

as well as I could."[9] We have, on the basis of that statement and on grounds of improved clarity, accepted several substantive readings from this edition;[10] but Southerne's "correcting" was far from careful or comprehensive, and C1 is generally less correct than Q1.[11]

In 1721, there was a second collected edition of the *Works*,[12] with *Oroonoko* (C2)[13] set from C1. We have also collated a later edition, a single sexto of 1736 (S),[14] which derives from one or the other of the two collected editions and illustrates a slight deterioration of the text.

In the prologue to Thomas Southerne's last tragedy, *The Spartan Dame* (1719), Elijah Fenton, who had earlier published a lengthy epistle in praise of the dramatist, depicted him as a remnant of an earlier age:

> *He comes, ambitious in his green Decline,*
> *To consecrate his Wreath at Beauty's Shrine.*
> *His* Oroonoko *never fail'd to engage*
> *The radiant Circles of the former Age:*
> *Each Bosom heav'd, all Eyes were seen to flow,*
> *And sympathize with* Isabella's *Woe.*[15]

This coupling of protagonists from Southerne's earlier successful tragedies, *The Fatal Marriage* (1694) and *Oroonoko* (1696), remained constant throughout the eighteenth century, during

9. Volume 1, sig. A2r.

10. See, especially, the textual notes to the following lines: I.i.191 (comic intensification); II.iii.79.4 (new information); and IV.i.15.

11. See, for example, the textual notes to the following lines: Dedication. 1. 24; I.i.167; I.i.211; I.i.223; I.ii.187; IV.i.236; and IV.i.247.

12. "*LONDON:* Printed for *J. Tonson, B. Tooke, M. Wellington,/* and *W. Chetwood.*"

13. 2: [177]–[266]. C2 is described: [H5r]–M1v in twelves. Copy collated: CLC, *PR3699/S3A1/1721.

14. "Printed for W. FEALES." S is described: [A1r]–[H5v] in sixes; viii, 9–92, [2]; [A1r] blank; [A1v] engraving of V.v; [A2r] title page advertisements for Benjamin Motte [H5r] and for Richard Wellington et al. [H5v].

15. *The Works of Mr. Thomas Southerne* (London, 1721), 2: 345. The two volumes of this edition (designated C2 above) will be cited henceforth as *Works*. See also Elijah Fenton, *An Epistle to Mr. Southerne* (London, 1711).

which both the plays continued prominently in the repertory.[16] Though both were altered to suit the taste of the more proper and sentimental second half of the century, they were still recognizable as the product of Southerne's unique talent. In the prologue to Southerne's last play, *Money the Mistress* (1726), Leonard Welsted could not resist referring to these two monuments to Southerne's fame:

> That Beauty, he has taught so oft to moan!
> That never let *Imoinda* weep alone,
> And made his *Isabella*'s Griefs its own![17]

Thus Southerne's reputation was tied to a particular kind of pathetic tragedy—a type that seemed, at the time, especially attractive to the ladies in the audience. An anonymous satirist remarked in 1703 that Southerne's "Heroes never fail to please the Fair,"[18] and Ramble, one of the speakers in *A Comparison between the Two Stages* (1702), responded to the mention of *Oroonoko* with "Oh! the Favourite of the Ladies."[19]

There is little doubt that when *Oroonoko* was first performed

16. According to *The London Stage*, there were at least 315 performances of *Oroonoko* and 188 of *The Fatal Marriage* (including its revision as *Isabella*) during the Restoration and eighteenth century. John Genest reports 17 performances of *Oroonoko* before 1830, of which Kean's, reviewed by William Hazlitt in *The Examiner* of 26 January 1817, was the most famous. Perhaps the first professional performance since Junius Brutus Booth revived the piece in New York in 1832 was staged on 3 August 1932 at the Malvern Festival, with Ralph Richardson in the leading role.

In assessing the popularity of *Oroonoko*, we should remember that it was one of a select group of dramas written during the Restoration that continued on the stage during the late eighteenth and early nineteenth centuries. *Oroonoko* was particularly popular as a play for visiting dignitaries, for benefit performances, and for introducing young new actors to the London theater.

17. (London, 1726), [sig. A3v]. For similar praise of Southerne's "admirable Talent for touching the Passions," see John Dennis, "Preface," *Liberty Asserted* (London, 1704), sig. a3.

18. *Religio Poetae: or, A Satyr on the Poets* (1703), quoted in John Wendell Dodds, *Thomas Southerne Dramatist*, Yale Studies in English, vol. 81 (New Haven, 1933), p. 7.

19. *A Comparison between the Two Stages*, ed. Staring B. Wells (Princeton, 1942), p. 19.

sometime in November 1695,[20] it was a considerable success, though there is no report of the premiere. *The Gentleman's Journal*, which had commented so favorably on *The Fatal Marriage*, had discontinued publication by November 1694, and theatrical information for the following two years is scanty. Charles Gildon's revision of Langbaine gives what is probably the best contemporary account of the play's reception, though he is so much taken up with praising his dead friend, Aphra Behn, from whose novella *Oroonoko* Southerne borrowed his main plot, that he hardly has space to comment on the play:

> But as to this Play of *Oroonoko*, you find our Poet has allow'd the Plot of it Mrs. *Behn's*; for on that Prince she has compos'd the best of her Novels: and as it must be confess'd that the Play had not its mighty Success without an innate Excellence; so in my Opinion, the necessary regularities a Dramatick Poet is obliged to observe, has left many Beauties in the Novel, which our Author cou'd not transfer to his Poem. As Mrs. *Barrey* did the Poet all the Justice so admirable an Actress, when she most exerts her self, could do, in the *Innocent Adultery*; so Mr. *Verbruggen*, in the Part of *Oroonoko*, by doing the Author Right, got himself the Reputation of one of the best Actors of his time.[21]

20. The exact date of the first performance is not known, but the likely publication date of 16 December 1695 (see above) can at least be used to suggest a November premiere since in the 1690s the usual lapse of time between initial performance of a play and its publication is about one month, and even less time "is quite common" (Judith Milhous and Robert D. Hume, "Dating Play Premières from Publication Data, 1660–1700," *Harvard Library Bulletin*, 23 [October 1974]: 394–97). In a letter dated 21 January 1696, John Oldmixon referred to *Oroonoko* as a play performed "about two Months ago," which may suggest the latter part of November rather than the beginning. See *The London Stage*, Part 1, ed. William Van Lennep (Carbondale, Ill., 1965), pp. 454–55, and Oldmixon, *Poems on Several Occasions* (London, 1696), p. 106.

21. *The Lives and Characters of the English Dramatic Poets* (London, [1699?]), p. 136. John Oldmixon, criticizing plays of the two theaters, remarked: "The Old House about two Months ago, made amends for the fatigues of a whole Winter; they gave us *Oroonoko*, a Tragedy, written by Mr. *Southern*, with as much purity and force, as any we have yet had from that Great Man. I cant say 'tis Regular

Gildon raises some side matters which will be taken up later, but his point about the "mighty Success" of the play and the excellent acting should be taken seriously. Indeed, the author of *A Comparison between the Two Stages* has one of his speakers refer to it as one of three "Masterpieces" that kept Drury Lane afloat during the 1690s.[22]

Often roles were created specifically to suit the talents of a particular performer, and the extent to which actresses like Barry, Bracegirdle, and Mrs. Verbruggen and actors of the caliber of Betterton, Mountfort, and Mr. Verbruggen influenced the shaping of stage characters was considerable. Verbruggen, who played Oroonoko, was accustomed to act the role of an heroic figure torn between passions of love and honor or, by the 1690s, tenderness and honor. His wife, the former Susanna Percival Mountfort, excelled in breeches roles like that of Charlotte Welldon. Tony Aston remarks that she was nevertheless reluctant to play Charlotte because she had "thick Legs and Thighs, corpulent and large Posteriors," but she had already acted such a role as the title character in Southerne's *Sir Anthony Love*.[23]

At the start of April 1695, Betterton moved from Drury Lane to Lincoln's Inn Fields, taking with him some of the best performers of the time, including Elizabeth Barry and Anne Bracegirdle. What effect such a move may have had on Southerne's conception of his play is difficult to say. Mrs. Verbruggen assumed the part of the leading comic actress of Rich's company at Drury Lane, and Frances Knight, who had acted a variety of lesser roles in the United Company, now tended to act the part of the villainess, although as the Widow Lackitt in *Oroonoko*

---

enough, but had it been more Correct, we should not easily have known which of Mr. *Otways* Plays to prefer before it" (*Poems on Several Occasions*, p. 106).

The novella *Oroonoko; Or The Royal Slave* by Aphra Behn (1640–89) was first published in 1688 in London; all quotations here are from Volume 5 of *The Works of Aphra Behn*, ed. Montague Summers (London, 1915; reissued New York: Benjamin Blom, 1967), and will be cited as Behn, *Works*, 5.

22. P. 20.

23. See Anthony Aston, *A Brief Supplement to Colley Cibber*, in *An Apology for the Life of Mr. Colley Cibber* (London, 1889), 2: 315, and John Harold Wilson, *All the King's Ladies* (Chicago, 1958), pp. 177–81.

she was also playing a character not very different from the long-suffering wife, Julia, which she acted in Southerne's *The Fatal Marriage*. On the other hand, the role of Imoinda, which went to Jane Rogers, might well have gone to the much more celebrated Barry or Bracegirdle before the split in the United Company.

Because of its heroic poignancy as well as the skill of the actors and actresses who played in it, *Oroonoko* remained popular througout the eighteenth and into the nineteenth century; but, as with *The Fatal Marriage*, critics increasingly protested the original blend of comic and tragic plots. As early as 1702, Sullen, in *A Comparison between the Two Stages*, after reproving Ramble for mouthing the cliché about *Oroonoko's* popularity only with women, adds, " 'tis . . . certain, that the Comick Part is below that Author's usual Genius."[24] By the middle of the century, a writer in *The Gentleman's Magazine* complained that the mixture of the tragic and the comic in *Oroonoko* was "absurd and most unnatural." He concluded that, "much against his inclination," Southerne had been forced to appease the taste of his times. "By introducing an under plot of the comic kind, though complete in all its parts, by exhibiting mirth in one scene and distress in another, our attention is too much diverted from the main story, and our concern for those who suffer too much weakened by such quick transitions."[25]

In 1759, the original *Oroonoko* was altered by John Hawkesworth, who cut out the comic scenes as being "loose and contemptible . . . , its mere comic Merit [could not] be ranked higher than a Droll for a Fair, where its Immorality ought to prevent its Exhibition; but as it is connected with the tragic, it is in a still higher Degree preposterous."[26] Garrick was a

24. P. 19.

25. "Observations on the Tragedy of Oroonoko," *The Gentleman's Magazine* 22 (1752): 163. Similarly the Abbé Le Blanc, registering the commonplaces about English tragedy that were obligatory for travelers from France, remarked that "*Oroonoko* is one of those remarkable plays for true and pathetic pictures, which produce so great an effect: yet this tragedy would not be indur'd on our theatre, because of the low comedy that is intermix'd with it" (*Letters on the English and French Nations* [London, 1747], 2: 46).

26. *Oroonoko, A Tragedy, With Alterations* (London, 1759), p. v. The reviewer in *The Critical Review* remarked that alterations were

great success in Hawkesworth's version, and in the following year Francis Gentleman printed his own altered version, with a prologue lamenting Southerne's misfortune to have lived and written in "an Age remarkable for wit and vice."[27] In that same year, 1760, an anonymous rewriter of *Oroonoko* (revisions of the play were apparently becoming a fad) complained that Southerne had "blended, with such truly Poetic Fire, Scenes beneath the lowest Farce."[28] Twenty-eight years later, John Ferriar adapted it as an anti-slave play with the title *The Prince of Angola*, and he too followed Hawkesworth in "rejecting the absurd, and insufferable underplot of the Old Play."[29] By 1817, Richard Cumberland was to complain that it was unbearable "that we should find ourselves in the company of such fellows as Jack Stanmore and Daniel Lackitt, each of them newly risen and reeking from a stye, that only hogs should wallow in, and hog-drivers describe."[30]

What this tells us is, to a certain extent, what, in general, we already know about the history of taste and particularly about the attack in the eighteenth and nineteenth centuries on the wit and sexual innuendo of Restoration drama; and it is not without its specific enlightening moments. Cumberland, for example, arrives at the original conclusion that Southerne is almost exclusively a writer for men rather than for women (contrary to the opinion of earlier critics), and he raises a question that is crucial in any consideration of Southerne: how, he asks, can Southerne "be at once so void of feeling, and yet so capable of exciting it; or, in other words, [how can it be] that an artist could bestow such workmanship upon so exquisite a gem, and

---

necessary, since the tragic action was interrupted by scenes of "the lowest buffoonery, and the grossest indecency" (*Critical Review*, 8 [1759]: 480–86).

The comic plot had already found its way into a droll called *The Sexes Mis-match'd; Or a New Way to get a Husband* (London, 1741; item 6 in a collection, *The Strollers Pacquet Open'd* [London, 1742]), in which the scene is shifted to Gibralter where Winlove (Charlotte) and Mrs. Lonfort (Lackitt) carry on their intrigue amidst scenes borrowed from Fletcher's *Monsieur Thomas*.

27. *Oroonoko: or the Royal Slave* (Glasgow, 1760), p. 7.
28. *Oroonoko* (London, 1760), p. iii.
29. *The Prince of Angola* (Manchester, 1788), p. ii.
30. *The British Drama* (London, 1817), 11: iv.

inclose it in a setting which no cleanly hand can touch."[31] Modern readers might well feel less queasy about the comic parts of *Oroonoko* than did eighteenth-century ones, but even they might wonder at the juxtaposition of a cuckolding farce with a tragedy somewhat reminiscent of *Othello* in its intensity. Southerne does not give us "comic relief" in the manner of Shakespeare's porter in *Macbeth* or the grave diggers in *Hamlet*; rather there seem to exist substantial comic and tragic worlds that occasionally touch but somehow never mesh.

Southerne is hardly unique in such treatment of parallel plots; this was a Restoration mode based on Renaissance models. Dryden's *Marriage à la Mode*, for instance, combines a cuckolding farce with a plot of *précieuse* love between royalty. But where Southerne's play differs from Dryden's earlier tragi-comic plays is in its tendency to draw the tragic plot down from the realm of artificial, *précieuse* heroic drama to a more human level. In following the new mode of a tragedy of "concernment," he was very much a disciple of the Thomas Otway of *The Orphan* and the later Dryden of *Don Sebastian*.[32] Yet the texture of *Oroonoko* is ultimately different from that of either of Southerne's masters. Southerne gives us the sense that tragic actions occur at precisely the same time that, somewhere else, there is comedy and laughter. The tragedies of Isabella in *The Fatal Marriage* and of Oroonoko and Imoinda are personal and dignified. One might think that the possibility of comedy entering at any moment would cause an effect that was closer to the sad than the tragic, but Southerne's heroes and heroines force us to acknowledge their tragic stature. Isabella establishes her situation through her speeches as a cosmic drama by means of a wealth of imagery drawn from the stars and a vaguely pagan underworld; Oroonoko by blank-verse proclamation simply demands that we acknowledge his dignity and greatness.

To a modern reader such tragic intensity combined with farce might appear to have ironic overtones such as Auden suggests in his "Musée des Beaux Arts":

31. Ibid.
32. See Eric Rothstein, *Restoration Tragedy* (Madison, 1967), pp. 16–20.

> About suffering they were never wrong,
> The old Masters: how well they understood
> Its human position; how it takes place
> While someone else is eating or opening a
>   window or just walking dully along.[33]

There is much to support such an interpretation. In *The Fatal Marriage*, the disastrous reappearance of Isabella's first husband, seemingly from the dead, and the trick played on Fernando to make him think that he has died and returned to earth after a day in purgatory, have an obvious and witty parallelism. No elements in *Oroonoko* are so dramatically symmetrical; but there is in it a clear parallel between the institution of slavery and the institution of marriage. That the question of liberty in marriage belongs to the arena of comedy and the same question in the matter of slavery to that of tragedy should not disguise their obvious connection.

The connection is more intellectual than dramatic, but the two plots are openly linked when Blanford asks Lucy and Charlotte Welldon to help save Oroonoko's life:

> So, Stanmore, you, I know, the women too,
> Will join with me.
>   (*To the women.*) 'Tis Oroonoko's cause,
> A lover's cause, a wretched woman's cause,
> That will become your intercession.
>
> (V.ii.11–14)

Oroonoko is a person capable of genuine love, a human being with great dignity, a king in his own country. But he is treated as a slave. The connection between the comic and the tragic plots, then, hinges on a relationship which we may appreciate and understand today, but which seemed either obscure or obscene to eighteenth-century critics. And the way in which the two actions are kept separate and distinct, except for an extremely witty association of ideas and themes, may have been something only the Restoration would have entirely admired.

---

33. *Collected Shorter Poems, 1927–1957* (New York: Random House, 1967), p. 123; reprinted by permission of the publisher.

The comic plot opens the play, with the story of the Welldon sisters, who have come husband-hunting to Surinam after embarassing, prolonged failure in London.[34] Their plight is presented in a comic fashion. Yet comedy, as Baudelaire reminds us, is something that happens to others, which, were it happening to ourselves, we would not find amusing at all.[35] Charlotte Welldon is witty about her situation, but she is not truly amused. And she has serious reasons for her feelings. The parallel with Oroonoko's situation is not merely that the Welldons are victims of a type of social injustice, but that women, like slaves, are treated as commodities, without regard for their humanity, their needs, or their desires.

Southerne had in fact already tried his hand at a play involving problems of women. But in *The Maid's Last Prayer*[36] the situation and characterization are traditional, the satire and anti-feminism integral to the plot; the object of derision is Lady Susan Malepert, the forty-five-year-old virgin who still acts like a young coquette. On the other hand, *Oroonoko*, opening as it does with a dialogue between two sophisticated and victimized women—instead of the usual formulaic repartee between rakes—suggests that here the women will at least have the first word in presenting their case against society. In a lengthy speech later in the play Charlotte Welldon complains of that double standard which reduces women's sexuality to the status of mercantile loss and gain:

> She would have a husband, and if all be as he says, she has no reason to complain; but there's no relying on what the men say upon these occasions. They have the benefit of their bragging by recommending their abilities to other women. Theirs is a trading estate that lives upon credit and increases by removing it out of one bank into another. Now poor women have not these opportunities. We must

34. The idea of America as a place where women, frustrated at home by men's refusal to marry them unless they had a fortune, might find husbands was still alive several decades later. See Daniel Defoe's comments in William Lee, *Daniel Defoe: His Life, and Recently Discovered Writings* (London, 1869), 2: 187–88.

35. "De L'Essence du Rire," *Oeuvres Complètes*, ed. Y. G. Le Dontec (Paris, 1961), p. 993.

36. (London, 1693).

keep our stocks dead by us at home to be ready for a purchase when it comes, a husband, let him be never so dear,
and be glad of him; or venture our fortunes abroad on such
rotten security that the principal and interest, nay, very
often our persons, are in danger. If the women would agree
(which they never will) to call home their effects, how many
proper gentlemen would sneak into another way of living
for want of being responsible in this? Then husbands would
be cheaper.   (IV.i.53–69)

Clearly, the lot of the women who could not find a man to marry
was unjust and desperate indeed. Women not only had the
disadvantage of having to wait until asked, but once married
were forced to relinquish the rights to their own property. Thus,
in the marriage market the emotional and economic advantages
lay entirely with the men.

Protests against the subordination of women were hardly
rare in the 1690s. Southerne earlier dramatized the desire of
one woman to break with the double standard in his *Sir Anthony
Love* (1691). In *An Essay upon Projects*, much of which was
written in 1693 and 1694, Defoe argued that women should be
as well educated as men, and in 1696 Mary Astell made her
passionate defense of women. Some of this pro-feminist literature had to do with the presence of an English queen on the
throne from the Revolution until her death in 1694. Yet an
informed awareness of the condition of women existed even
before 1688; and Queen Mary's influence cannot explain the
intensity of a Mary Astell or the sudden emergence of women
writers of some talent. Nor can it account for the scene in
Oroonoko when Charlotte has to remind Captain Driver that
women are not quite on the level of slaves, to be bought and
sold—at least not to be bought and sold "in public." An anonymous pamphlet of 1703, *The Levellers*, protested that "Matri-
mony is indeed become a meer Trade[.] They carry their
Daughters to *Smithfield* as they do Horses, and sell to the highest
bidder." The writer of this work proposed the abolition of dowries
and a tax on bachelors which would, in turn, provide compensa-
tion for married men and women with children.[37]

37. (London, 1703), pp. 3, 8–9.

Charlotte and Lucy Welldon are not untypical of some of the real women of the period, who left England to find a man in the colonies. Economics forced them, as it forced others, to pursue marriage by any means. They are realists; they frankly acknowledge what Southerne states epigrammatically in his epilogue to *The Maid's Last Prayer*:

> *Disguise your Inclinations as you can:*
> *Yet every Woman's Business is a Man.*

When the Widow Lackitt's son, Daniel, proves to be a fool of even greater dimensions than would be acceptable in the most flagrant marriage of convenience, he is brought to kneel before his wife, beg her forgiveness, and take an "oath of allegiance" which has sexual, financial, and political ramifications.[38] The desire of the Welldons at this point is not sexual license but marriage with some dignity. In this, the women find their justification in natural law[39] as opposed to the laws of a society which dictate obsequious waiting to the affluent and spinsterhood to the dowry-less.

That the Welldons are ultimately on the side of natural law in matters of love and marriage is yet another link between their lives and the lives of Oroonoko and Imoinda. It explains why they respond immediately to Blanford's plea, at that point in Act V where the two plots first meet openly, that they follow "Oroonoko's cause,/A lover's cause, a wretched woman's cause" (V.ii.12–13). But when the news of Oroonoko's uprising is first introduced to the Welldons, Lucy merely says: "There's something the matter too with the slaves, some disturbance or other; I don't know what 'tis" (IV.i.210–11), and Charlotte thinks of it

38. There was considerable comment on the relations between women and fools. In the Epilogue to his *The Wives Excuse* (1692), Southerne sums up the argument of the play, in his *"hints to Fools,"* that fools drive their wives to infidelity. But another view was that women deliberately selected fools for husbands or lovers in order to be unfaithful without arousing jealousy or suspicion. See Thomas Durfey, *The Marriage-Hater Match'd* (London, 1692), p. 37 (IV.i).

39. For some discussion of these matters, see Samuel Pufendorf, *Of the Law of Nature and Nations* (1672), trans. Basil Kennett (Oxford, 1703), Book 6, Chapter 1, Articles 21–22, pp. 90–92.

only as an advantage by which their devices may succeed the better. They are on Oroonoko's side, but his story is not theirs. His tragedy occurs simultaneously with but outside the comic conclusion of their lives in marriage.

There appears to be no single source for the comic plot of *Oroonoko*. John Dodds has hinted that a source may be found in Thomas Middleton's *No Wit, No Help Like a Woman's*, which was revised for the Restoration stage as *The Counterfeit Bridegroom: or, The Defeated Widow* in 1676 or 1677.[40] The exact reasons for this suggestion are not entirely clear, for there are certainly no verbal borrowings from either Middleton's original or the revised version. The only similarity to Middleton's plot is that Southerne's Charlotte Welldon in fact "marries" Widow Lackitt and substitutes a man, Jack Stanmore, to perform as a surrogate husband at night. But no one would think that Middleton had influenced Southerne's *Sir Anthony Love* (1690) in which the heroine, if one may call her that, arranges a secret marriage with Volante and plans to put Ilford, Volante's admirer, in her place to assume the role of the male lover. It is easier to credit the notion that Southerne embellished the idea from his own play than to conceive of any special indebtedness to Middleton.

On the other hand, the comic plot is certainly indebted to variations on the Restoration comic formulas involving breeches roles from Thomas Shadwell's *The Woman Captain* to Aphra Behn's *The Widow Ranter*. Betterton's Company in Lincoln's Inn Fields opened the season which produced *Oroonoko* with a play by a woman who signed herself "Ariadne," which began with the heroine, Charlot Frankford, and her cousin dressed in male attire. Charlot pursues Charles Lovewell, marries him and tests his love in much the same way that Charlotte Welldon makes sure of Stanmore's honor before deciding to venture with him into marriage.[41] Although there are thus many analogues to the comic plot, it would be futile to search for any single source.

While Southerne merely contributed delicate variations to the various plot formulas of Restoration comedy, he was famous

40. Dodds, p. 148.
41. See *She Ventures, and He Wins* (London, 1696).

in his own time for the "purity" of his language.[42] The author
of one panegyric, "To Mr. *Southerne*, on his Play, call'd, *The
Fatal Marriage*," suggested that Southerne succeeded in welding
together his comic and tragic segments by a similarity and fineness
of style:

> So fine your Passions; so sublime your Thought;
> All, ev'ry part, so exquisitely wrote;
> So short your Repartees, and yet so plain,
> That Criticks lose their old accustom'd Aim.
> Whilst others Blaze at distance, but when nigh
> Afford not half the pleasure to the Eye,
> You, like a well form'd Lamp, disperse your Rays
> With equal Lustre, round, in ev'ry Place.
> Great is our Joy, with wonder we look on,
> To see so fine a Texture, yet so strong.[43]

In the same manner, Ramble and Sullen, in *A Comparison
between the Stages*, praise his "Stile and agreeable Manner," his
"Spirit of Conversation," and the naturalness of his dialogue.
"But I must say," Sullen adds, "his Diction is commonly the best
part of him, especially in Comedy." Sullen's creator was probably
thinking more of comedies like *The Wive's Excuse* (1692) than
of *Oroonoko*, but even if the comic part of *Oroonoko* was considered "below that Author's usual Genius," it was still good
enough for the play to be regarded as one of the "Masterpieces"
of the Restoration stage.[44]

Southerne's excellence as a writer of comedies depended not
only on his style but also on a closely observed social context.
Like most playwrights of the 1690s, he provided an excess of
plot in order to free the comedy from the necessity of plot. As
in Congreve, there is a subtle interplay of character and a
sophisticated view of sexual desire as a moving force behind
society's social polish. The comic plot of *Oroonoko* is, however,

42. For a discussion of the meaning of the term "purity" as applied
to Southerne's drama, see Ralph R. Thornton, ed., *The Wives Excuse*
(Wynnewood, Pa., 1973), pp. 32–34. Thornton's interpretation suggests
a moral purity without dwelling sufficiently on a stylistic purity.

43. W. S., "To Mr. *Southerne*, on his play, call'd, *The Fatal Marriage*," in *The Fatal Marriage* (London, 1694), sig. A3v.

44. *Comparison between the Stages*, pp. 19–20.

different from those of the comedies of London life; it is in some ways, more like his last play, *Money the Mistress* (1726), which is set in Gibraltar. The comic action of *Oroonoko* takes place in Surinam, far from the complexities of London society. Without the involved social context of London, the comedy tends to be broader and more farcical. Only Charlotte Welldon seems to have escaped from London with some of her wit and intelligence intact. The Widow Lackitt is amusing, but she would do no better in London society than Aphra Behn's pipe-smoking, cursing Widow Ranter. And her foolish son Daniel has his parallel only in the lumpish young country squires trotted across the stage to be laughed at by the Restoration wits.

Montague Summers appears to be the only modern critic to find that *Oroonoko* possesses "an excellent comic underplot, full of humour and the truest *vis comica*."[45] But then he seems also to be the only critic who is not affronted by the seeming immorality of the Welldons' quest for husbands. The underplot is certainly a disappointment as a comedy of wit, but what Southerne needed as a contrast to Oroonoko's tragic love and outraged honor was a farce in which love was sex and honor contrivance. And in this strange blend of opposites he succeeded very well.

The tragic plot offers different problems. If we are not careful, we might lose our perspective on Oroonoko's tragedy not only by focusing too much on it from the Welldons' roving, inattentive view, but also by looking at it through a miasma of modern social attitudes. For example, we might tend to see it exclusively as a tragedy of the black slave in the new world. Yet John Ferriar, who revised *Oroonoko* into an anti-slavery play, *The Prince of Angola*, in 1788, complained that Southerne had, in fact, "delivered by the medium of his Hero, a grovelling apology for slave-holders . . . and an illiberal contempt of the unhappy Negroes is so entwined with the fabric of the Piece, that it was impossible to separate it, without making large encroachments on the Author's design."[46] To Ferriar, as to us,

45. Behn, *Works*, 5: 128. Summers has taken his opinion directly from John Genest, *Some Account of the English Stage* (Bath, 1832), 2: 71.
46. *Prince of Angola*, p. ii.

slavery is a "systematic inhumanity."[47] (Interestingly enough, however, Ferriar weakens Oroonoko's militancy by omitting his murder of the Governor at the end as indecorous.) Even so *The Prince of Angola* was banned in Liverpool in its day as were other versions of the play.[48] One age's liberalism may seem another's racism.

Ferriar's view of Southerne's play is much like that presented by Wylie Sypher in labelling an entire set of attitudes the "Oroonoko Legend." Oroonoko is the "Negro précieux" and Imoinda has an "air of the salon." Both are archetypes of the "noble Negro" as distinguished from the inferior Negro slaves who are hardly worth saving.[49] This fierce distinction between two "classes" of blacks is already present in Southerne's source in Aphra Behn.[50] It was also, no doubt, rigorously insisted upon in the staging of the play in physical attitude as well as in dress. An 1831 edition of the play shows, for example, that the actor playing Oroonoko was costumed in "black silk arms and leggings—red sandals—cream-coloured shirt and cloak, handsomely ornamented—rich belt—bracelets—gold band for the head." Aboan, on the other hand, was consigned to "black cotton arms and leggings" and the female slaves to "white cotton bedgowns and petticoats."[51]

This distinction between "worthy" and "inferior" or "equal" and "unequal" blacks is unacceptable to modern sensibilities, but if *Oroonoko* is not therefore the anti-slavery play we might wish it to be, neither is it a defense of the kind of slavery then practiced in the West Indies. Although the debate over slavery

47. Ibid., p. ix.
48. According to Mrs. Inchbald, "The tragedy of 'Oroonoko' is never acted in Liverpool, for the very reason why it ought to be acted there oftener than at any other place—The merchants of that great city acquire their riches by the slave trade" (*Oroonoko*, in *The British Theatre*, ed. Elizabeth Inchbald, 7 [London, 1808]: 4). The preface to the edition published in *Bell's British Theatre* (London, 1791) had made a similar assertion (no. 34, sig. Aiii). For statistics on Liverpool's importance as a center of the late eighteenth-century slave trade, see Basil Davidson, *The African Slave Trade* (Boston, 1961), pp. 60–68.
49. *Guinea's Captive Kings* (Chapel Hill, 1942), pp. 108–15.
50. Behn, *Works*, 5: 136.
51. *Oroonoko*, "Printed from the Acting Copy, with Remarks, Biographical and Critical, by D-G" (London, [1831]), p. 8.

had not reached the intensity it was to achieve after the middle of the eighteenth century, there was already no lack of awareness of the difficulties involved in a trade that treated human beings as commodities. Many an Englishman was captured and enslaved by Barbary pirates, and the life of the white indentured servant or the transported criminal in America was only slightly different from that of the black slave.[52] But it was the life of the black slave, captured, usually, by fellow Africans like Oroonoko and sold to the Europeans for transport to places like Surinam, Jamaica, or Virginia, that commanded most attention. George Warren, in a work that probably influenced Aphra Behn, described how, in Surinam,

> they are sold like Dogs, and no better esteem'd but for their Work sake, which they perform all the Week with the severest usages for the slightest fault. . . . These wretched miseries not seldome drive them to desperate attempts for the Recovery of their Liberty, endevouring to escape . . . or if the hope of Pardon bring them again alive into their Masters power, they'l manifest their fortitude, or rather obstinacy in suffering the most exquisite tortures can be inflicted upon them, for a terrour and example to others without shrinking.[53]

Similar accounts abound. Richard Ligon reported how black slaves brought to Barbados are sold "as they do Horses in a Market" at thirty pounds sterling for men, twenty-seven for women. He idealized their chastity, their trust in a God who will punish evil men, and, yes, their wonderful sense of rhythm. Ligon, like Warren, commented on slave revolts and on the fortitude of their leaders.[54] A dramatic revolt occurred on Jamaica in 1690, and sixty slaves were executed on Barbados for plotting an uprising.[55] Such rebellions did not prevent various writers from praising the slaves; even a follower of Hobbes

52. In Behn's *Oroonoko*, the narrator also refers to *"Indian Slaves."* See Behn, *Works*, 5: 188.

53. *An Impartial Description of Surinam* (London, 1667), p. 19.

54. *A Trve & Exact History of the Island of Barbadoes* (London, 1657), pp. 46–48.

55. Narcissus Luttrell, *A Brief Historical Relation of State Affairs* (Oxford, 1857), 2: 137; 3: 8, 13.

would have agreed that, given their status, they had a right to revolt when they could. And by 1695, writers like D'Olfert Dapper had impressed Europeans with the primitive virtues of the Africans, their obedience to the laws of nature and their freedom from the corruptions of European civilization.[56]

But the most moving case for the black slaves may be found in Thomas Tryon's *Friendly Advice to the Gentlemen-Planters of the East and West Indies*, published in 1684. Although a good case has been made for Behn's knowledge of this work,[57] the oratorical and dialogue forms employed by Tryon and his continual underscoring of the unchristian behavior of the planters may have provided Southerne with some extra hints as well. Tryon's Negro remarks that the law of nature itself urges the slaves to run away; yet, if they are caught, they are burned alive. He exclaims, "O thou most just and eternal Lawgiver, and Perswader of all Creatures! Do these things taste or savour of Christianity?"[58] Tryon's Negro slave has the eloquence frequently attributed to noble savages and barbarians in the literature of the seventeenth and eighteenth centuries. In the third part, in a "Dialogue" between another slave, Sambo, and his Master, Sambo goes as far as to justify revolt and to threaten the plantation owners with the same fate as the Spaniards, whose empire, built on the blood of slaughtered Indians, went into a rapid decline.[59]

Tryon, of course, did not argue against slavery itself, but rather against the cruelties practiced on the slaves. Of the three adaptations of Southerne's tragedy published around 1760, Hawkesworth's omitted anything that might be taken as an attack on the planters or on the institution of slavery, and Gentleman's, in spite of a few added speeches on liberty and

56. D'Olfert Dapper, *Description de l'Afrique* (Amsterdam, 1686), pp. 234–38. No general slave insurrection occurred in Surinam until 1730. See Philip Hanson Hiss, *Netherlands America* (New York, 1943), p. 88.

57. Ruthe T. Sheffey, "Some Evidence for a New Source of Aphra Behn's *Oroonoko*," *Studies in Philology* 59 (1962): 52–63.

58. (London, 1684), p. 112. Some writers argued against making the slaves Christians on the grounds that to do so would mean that they had to be freed, but Morgan Godwyn argued that this was only an excuse to continue their cruelties. See Godwyn, *A Supplement to the Negro's & Indian's Advocate* (London, 1681), pp. 5–10.

59. Tryon, pp. 203–4, 212.

on the natural virtues of the slaves, refused to commit itself. Only the anonymous version of 1760 directly attacks slavery as an unacceptable solution to the need for labor in the colonies.[60] As for Southerne, modern readers and playgoers will find many of his views unpalatable; yet despite the portrayal of a cowardly slave like Hottman and Blanford's seemingly approved vision of the majority of slaves as naturally inferior creatures, Southerne still makes the Lieutenant Governor and his followers among the planters the unmistakable villains of the piece.

But if we are to go so far, it might be worth seeing *Oroonoko* in terms of Southerne's own high Tory politics.[61] The image of a prince like Oroonoko kidnapped by a ruffian like Captain Driver and faced by a group of planters who applaud the traitorous actions of the Captain as revealing the promise of one "fit to be employed in public affairs" is similar to Southerne's numerous depictions of a rabble incapable of comprehending

60. Imoinda asks Maria, a character introduced by the anonymous reviser, how England can permit the sale of Negroes in her colonies:

> This more than savage Right, of thus disposing,
> Like th' marketable Brute, their Fellow-Creatures Blood?
> Whose equal Rectitude of fair Proportion—
> Their strong Intelligence—their Aptitude,
> In Reason's Rules, loudly, nay, terribly pronounce,
> They stand the equal Work of Reason's God.

On the other hand, Blanford argues that most of the slaves would have been killed in the wars in Africa were it not for the profit that could be gained from their sale. See *Oroonoko* (London, 1760), pp. 5–6, 42.

61. Although Southerne accepted Whig patronage after 1688, there is no reason to think that in the plays written after the Glorious Revolution he revised the aristocratic assumptions that inform his earlier plays. He was accused of changing sides ("turning cat in the pan"), but the evidence presented by Clifford Leech suggests little more than a switch from Jacobite to Tory. Professor George Guffey has argued that Behn's novella itself may be read partly as a political document in favor of James II, and some of Behn's attitudes toward the colonists in Virginia may have entered into Southerne's picture of the planters of Surinam. See Guffey, "Aphra Behn's *Oroonoko:* Occasion and Accomplishment," in *Two English Novelists* (Los Angeles: Wm. Andrews Clark Memorial Library, 1975); Behn, *The Widow Ranter: or, the History of Bacon in Virginia*, in Behn, *Works*, 4: 232–37 (I.i); and Clifford Leech, "The Political 'Disloyalty' of Thomas Southerne," *Modern Language Review* 28 (1933): 430.

the nature of monarchy, nobility, or anything but immediate, material gain.[62] Southerne would seem to imply that men like Oroonoko are natural rulers and the planters typical subjects, incapable of either ruling or selecting a ruler. Wylie Sypher was closer to the truth than Ferrier when he argued that Southerne's theme was the depravity of the white man.[63] To be more precise, if we are to regard Oroonoko as Southerne's ideal, we must also assume that he is commenting on the moral cowardice of a large part of mankind, both white and black.

Southerne wrote his play after the Glorious Revolution of 1688, but what one historian has called the "Financial Revolution," which was to some extent the product of the political revolution, was just beginning.[64] This is the era that Robert Gould satirized in his poem, *The Corruption of the Times by Money*,[65] and Stanmore's remark that "great estates" are raised by the methods of a Captain Driver was not without its contemporary significance. It is a period which can appreciate a hero only so long as he is useful; once Oroonoko has preserved the colony from the Indians, the planters see no value, no use, in his heroic virtues.[66]

In his contempt for the commercial classes, and in his admiration for the "Liberty" preached by Oroonoko, Southerne shows something of the same attitude taken by John Dryden after the departure of James II had ended the conservative myth of absolute monarchy in England.[67] It was an attitude that led to the ambiguities of the "politics of nostalgia" in the next century.[68] Insofar as slavery was viewed as a product of the capitalist men-

62. See, for example, *The Loyal Brother* (1682) in *Works*, 1: 58–62 (V.ii); and *The Fate of Capua* (1700), in *Works*, 2: 278–81 (I.ii).

63. Sypher, *Guinea's Captive Kings*, p. 116.

64. P. G. M. Dickson, *The Financial Revolution in England* (London, 1967), pp. 1–75.

65. (London, 1693), pp. 1–30.

66. For a similar situation, see *The Widow Ranter*, in Behn, *Works*, 4: 230–37 (I.i–ii).

67. See, for example, "To My Honour'd Kinsman, John Driden," *The Poems of John Dryden*, ed. James Kinsley (Oxford, 1958), 4: 1534, ll. 184–94.

68. We take the term from Isaac Kramnick's *Bolingbroke and His Circle: The Politics of Nostalgia in the Age of Walpole* (Cambridge, 1968).

tality, it was frequently attacked by men like Southerne. No wonder, then, that Samuel Johnson drank a toast at Oxford to "the next insurrection of the negroes in the West Indies" and regarded the American slaveholders' patriotic speeches on liberty with contempt.[69]

We should remain aware, then, of the contemporary significance of the play, but Southerne was writing drama, not a tract for the times; we must turn to the play itself to see how these ideas emerge in the interplay of character and dialogue.

When the slaves are brought out for sale, Stanmore tells Lucy that not only the slaves but all their offspring will pass their lives in servitude. When Lucy exclaims, "O miserable fortune!" Blanford responds, "Most of 'em know no better; they were born so and only change their masters. But a prince, born only to command, betrayed and sold! My heart drops blood for him" (I.ii.190–93). In a dramatic sense Blanford's view is not intended to obliterate Lucy's passionate exclamation from the minds of the audience; it merely shifts the focus.[70] The slaves singing to divert Clemene are given the same weight as the shepherds and shepherdesses of pastoral or the Incas and Aztecs of heroic tragedy. They are innocents and possess greater moral weight than the low-minded planters who mistreat them. When Hottman complains about suffering "under the bloody whip" (III.i.9), he is conjuring up images of cruelty which are never entirely removed or justified.

If Hottman proves to be a demagogue, what are we to think of Oroonoko's high-flown rhetoric which leads the slaves to rebel or of their human failings in surrendering to their white enemies at the persuasion of their wives? And what are we to think of Aboan, Oroonoko's "slave," who dies heroically at his master's feet after suffering terrible tortures? Among the blacks, there are

69. James Boswell, *Boswell's Life of Johnson*, ed. George Birkbeck Hill and L. F. Powell (Oxford, 1934), 3: 200–201.

70. Although we may have lost that particular focus on the play, it should be remarked that eighteenth-century critics admired Blanford as a truly benevolent character. See "Observations on the Tragedy of Oroonoko," *The Gentleman's Magazine*, 22 (1752): 166–67. In the anonymous revision of 1760, he is made into a sentimental lover and a man of benevolent spirit. See *Oroonoko* (London, 1760), pp. 42–43.

indeed Hottmans and men of only moderate courage, but all along we are reminded that none of them has had the benefits of Western religion and culture.

Oroonoko himself, of course, is anything but an ordinary slave. Not only is he a prince, but he has been turned into a slave through Captain Driver's violation of all ties of friendship and hospitality. In his own country, Oroonoko dealt with slave traders for the men he captured in battle, and he sees nothing inherently wrong with the idea of slavery itself. We should not be surprised, then, that in his anger at the failure of the slaves to remain loyal to him in his rebellion, he should use the language of the apologists for slavery, calling them "beasts" only lacking tails (IV.ii.56–72). When Aboan argues that Oroonoko must think of freeing himself, his master's first response is to argue that the slaves have been purchased by the "honest way of trade." Captain Driver may break through the ties between men that make for commerce, but he, Oroonoko, will not show such "black ingratitude" as to violate the planters' rights of "property" (III.ii.101–13). It is a neat psychological touch on Southerne's part that Oroonoko should falsely associate his privileged treatment with that received by the other slaves and argue, "We ought not to complain" (III.ii.119). Unmoved by Aboan's description of the sufferings of other slaves, he is, however, immediately aroused by the prospect of his future son being born a slave. Drawing upon the psychology of the heroic play, Southerne accompanies Oroonoko's heroic qualities with a dangerous egotism.

In his tendency to self-dramatization, Oroonoko suffers from an incapacity to grasp what is really happening around him. For example, there are considerable warnings that the slaves he inspires to revolt will fail him in the end. One of them reminds him of all the problems involved, of the children and women who must suffer from such an act. Oroonoko dismisses such an objection with an heroic sweep. In his vision of a paradisical colony, the grandeur of his concept is matched by its impracticality.

> Therefore I still propose to lead our march
> Down to the sea and plant a colony
> Where, in our native innocence, we shall live
> Free and be able to defend ourselves

Till stress of weather or some accident
Provide a ship for us.
(III.iv.23–28)

With this kind of grand, sentimental utopianism we need the comic subplot to keep our feet planted in reality.

Oroonoko's tragedy is that of a man whose greatness has little connection with the lives of those around him. His love for Imoinda is presented as an all-consuming passion, just as it would be for any lover in a novella of the period. If Behn's novella is very different from works like *The Noble Slave*, it is mostly so in its barbaric ending with the violent deaths of the pregnant Imoinda and Oroonoko. But Southerne would have found material in her ending which would not have been very different from the plays he had written or was to write about the Greeks and Romans. By removing some of Behn's details, he gives Oroonoko the status of those who, in *The Fall of Capua* and *The Spartan Dame*, react violently to the idea of their loved ones being ravished. As Cleombrotus ravishes his sister-in-law and violates his code of honor in *The Spartan Dame*, so the Lieutenant Governor in *Oroonoko* attempts to ravish Imoinda and betrays his virtue as a Christian and as the leader of the colony.[71] In short, what we have in *Oroonoko* is a typical Southerne tragedy of nobility in the face of betrayal and of virtue outraged or nearly outraged by lust. Oroonoko, himself, is a cross between a noble and stoic Greek or Roman and a noble savage of the Almanzor vintage.

The single major source for Southerne's play is Aphra Behn's *Oroonoko: or, The Royal Slave*, published in either late 1688 or early 1689. The general outlines of the plots are similar, though Southerne's dramatic presentation gives the characters very different form. There is nothing in Behn's novella to suggest the comic plot of the play, unless one chooses to think that in the militant feminism of the Welldon sisters there is some reflection of Aphra Behn herself, or, at least, of the book's bold feminine first-person narrator. But in Behn's "Eye-witness" to

71. Since *The Spartan Dame* was written before 1688, Southerne's particular tendency to a tragedy of this nature was formed before *Oroonoko*. See *Works*, 2: 341.

the events in Surinam, there is little of the feminist who claimed elsewhere that her plays were discriminated against simply because she was a woman.[72] The play contains some changes in detail: the Lieutenant Governor identified as Byam in the novella goes nameless in the play, and the part taken by a Mr. Trefry in Behn's work is given to Blanford in Southerne. More significantly, Imoinda, Behn's "black Venus," is transformed into a beautiful white girl by Southerne.[73] Rather than a Prince of Coromantien, Oroonoko is made the Prince of Angola. Aboan disappears early in the novella, and a slave named Tuscan is introduced toward the end as Oroonoko's loyal follower. No Hottman or Aboan persuades Oroonoko to revolt in Behn's work; it is all his own idea. And at the end, Behn's hero is kept alive after killing Imoinda and an Englishman (not the Lieutenant Governor), only to suffer a terrible death through the slow dismemberment of his parts, ears, nose, and arms, while he stoically smokes his pipe until dead.[74]

As might be expected, Southerne's main task is to change telling into showing—to change prose fiction into drama. He makes the plot more concise and gives his characters voices which otherwise they do not have. For the most part, Aphra Behn's hero speaks in a manner barely distinguishable from the heroes of other contemporary novellas or from the other characters in her *Oroonoko*. Southerne gives him a particular voice—dignified, simple, ironic, passionate. Othello comes to mind, but Oroonoko's smoldering resentment and terse phrase is unique. He is always

72. See Behn, *Works*, 3: 129, 183–87.
73. Wylie Sypher (*Guinea's Captive Kings*, p. 21) suggests that Imoinda, "more acceptably" for theater audiences, was a white, but this is not apparent to all of Southerne's contemporaries. He was attacked for failing to give Imoinda, born in "an *Indian* Air,/ . . . an *Indian* Hue," in "The Tryall of Skill," ed. Frank H. Ellis (New Haven, 1970), 6: 708. Surely Southerne's audience would have had little more difficulty admiring a beautiful African princess than a handsome African prince. The change in Oroonoko's native land may have been made for historical accuracy (Angola was famous for its "grand trafic d'Esclaves"), or because the Coromantiens had a reputation for savagery. See Nicolas Sanson, *L'Afrique* (Paris, 1656), p. 68; and Wylie Sypher, "A Note on the Realism of Mrs. Behn's *Oroonoko*," *Modern Language Quarterly* 3 (1942): 401–5.
74. For some further comparisons, see Dodds, pp. 133–35.

Oroonoko, whether he is commenting on Blanford's decision to call him Caesar, "I am myself, but call me what you please" (I.ii.262), or roaring out his most famous rant:

> Ha! Thou has roused
> The lion in his den; he stalks abroad
> And the wide forest trembles at his roar.
> I find the danger now; my spirits start
> At the alarm and from all quarters come
> To man my heart, the citadel of love.
> Is there a pow'r on earth to force you from me?
> And shall I not resist it? Not strike first
> To keep, to save you? To prevent that curse?
> This is your cause, and shall it not prevail?
> O! You were born all ways to conquer me.
> (III.ii.205–15)

A good comparison between Behm's prose and Southerne's blank verse may be found in his adaptation of the scene in which Oroonoko replies to the objections of the slaves, particularly to one concerned for the safety of the women and children who will have to accompany the men in their rebellion. This is Behn's version:

> After this he would have proceeded, but was interrupted by a tall *Negro*, of some more Quality than the rest, his Name was *Tuscan*; who bowing at the Feet of *Caesar*, cry'd, "My Lord, we have listen'd with Joy and Attention to what you have said; and, were we only Men, would follow so great a Leader through the World: But O! consider we are Husbands and Parents too, and have Things more dear to us than Life; our Wives and Children, unfit for Travel in those unpassable Woods, Mountains and Bogs. We have not only difficult Lands to overcome, but Rivers to wade, and Mountains to encounter; ravenous Beasts of Prey."— *To this* Caesar *reply'd*, "That Honour was the first Principle in Nature, that was to be obey'd; but as no Man would pretend to that, without all the Acts of Virtue, Compassion, Charity, Love, Justice and Reason, he found it not inconsistent with that, to take equal Care of their Wives and Children as they would of themselves; and that he did

not design, when he led them to Freedom, and glorious Liberty, that they should leave that better Part of themselves to perish by the Hand of the Tyrant's Whip: But if there were a Woman among them so degenerate from Love and Virtue, to chuse Slavery before the Pursuit of her Husband, and with the Hazard of her Life, to share with him in his Fortunes; that such a one ought to be abandoned, and left as a Prey to the common Enemy."[75]

Southerne positions it at the start of the fourth scene of act three, with Oroonoko's impassioned response to an objection we have not heard:

> Impossible! Nothing's impossible.
> We know our strength only by being tried.
> If you object the mountains, rivers, woods
> Unpassable that lie before our march:
> Woods we can set on fire, we swim by nature.
> What can oppose us then, but we may tame?
> All things submit to virtuous industry;
> That we can carry with us, that is ours.

SLAVE.

> Great sir, we have attended all you said
> With silent joy and admiration
> And, were we only men, would follow such,
> So great a leader, through the untried world.
> But, O! Consider we have other names,
> Husbands and fathers, and have things more dear
> To us than life, our children and our wives,
> Unfit for such an expedition.
> What must become of them?

OROONOKO.   We wonnot wrong
> The virtue of our women to believe
> There is a wife among 'em would refuse
> To share her husband's fortune. What is hard
> We must make easy to 'em in our love. While we live
> And have our limbs, we can take care for them;
> Therefore I still propose to lead our march

75. Behn, *Works*, 5: 191–92.

Down to the sea and plant a colony
Where, in our native innocence, we shall live
Free and be able to defend ourselves
Till stress of weather or some accident
Provide a ship for us.

It should be clear that in adapting the little dialogue that Behn provides, Southerne gave each of his characters a distinct poetic language. All that might be heroic and grand is given to Oroonoko, leaving Southerne's nameless slave only the pathetic concern about his family.

Behn uses far more specific descriptive detail than Southerne, treating everything from the fauna and flora of Surinam to the gruesome deaths of the hero and heroine. Imoinda is not merely stabbed, as in Southerne; she has her throat cut and her head removed ("then severing her yet smiling Face from that delicate Body, pregnant as it was with the Fruits of tenderest Love"),[76] to the accompaniment of the florid style of the contemporary novella.[77] We are told how Imoinda's body then begins to decay and "stink," and when Oroonoko is finally found by the white planters, he attempts to kill himself by cutting a piece of flesh from his throat, slicing open his belly and pulling out his bowels.[78] The combination of realistic action and *précieuse* style in Behn produces an effect that is grotesque. Southerne's hero and heroine are more Spartan than barbaric. No indecorous realism destroys the noble impact of Oroonoko's private sufferings. As in classical tragedy, Aboan, acting the traditional role of a messenger, enters to tell of his own torments and of the terrible tortures that await Oroonoko. A French critic in Southerne's audience would have found enough violence and death in *Oroonoko* to comment on the artistic errors of English tragedy, but Southerne stopped far short of depicting on the

76. Behn, *Works*, 5: 203.
77. For a discussion of style and its complications in contemporary "novels," particularly those translated from the French, see Maximillian E. Novak, "Fiction and Society in the Early Eighteenth Century," in *England in the Restoration and Early Eighteenth Century*, ed. H. T. Swedenberg, Jr. (Berkeley, 1972), pp. 51–64.
78. Behn, *Works*, 5: 202–8.

stage such episodes as the brutal disembowelment in Behn.[79] Oroonoko dies with dignity, having achieved the revenge on the Lieutenant Governor which he wanted but could not achieve in Behn's novella. When, toward the end, he tells the Governor's men who discover him with his dead Imoinda, "Put up your swords," we are again reminded of Othello, but he is like no one so much as Dryden and Southerne's own Cleomenes, who dies lamenting that there is no one in all Egypt worthy enough for him to fight.[80]

Although the tragic and the comic actions do not impinge on each other in any direct way, it is the strongly worked cross-cutting or juxtaposition of the two which gives Southerne's play its scope and dramatic impact. Neither his source in Behn nor the later alterations of his play employ this central technique of structure and tone. It is perhaps the nature of drama in general and of seventeenth-century drama in particular to establish its "presence" by this oscillation. If Charlotte Welldon is the leader of the comic action and Oroonoko the chief personage of the noble action, it is surely Imoinda who is used by Southerne to coordinate and bind the two plot lines in their themes and concerns. As a woman and as a slave who is captive of both the English and the Indians and as the European wife of an Angolan prince, she embodies the two principal thematic dualities of slaves/women and European/"barbarian" which give the play its intellectual force. Whereas in Behn the Lieutenant Governor acts out of a generalized malevolence, in Southerne his lust for Imoinda motivates his treachery toward Oroonoko. It is the pressure of her pregnancy which stirs Oroonoko to revolt; her nobility helps to confirm his greatness. And, in turn,

79. For a typical continental view of violence and death on the English stage, see Béat Louis de Muralt, *Letters Describing The Character and Customs of the English and French Nations* (London, 1726), p. 30. A later French observer, the Abbé le Blanc, praised *Oroonoko* for its pathos, and it did have some influence on the continent. See Edward D. Seeber, "Oroonoko in France in the Eighteenth Century," *PMLA* 51 (1936): 953–59.

80. Although Southerne was obviously much influenced by Shakespeare, Dodds tends to overstate the "Elizabethan" nature of Southerne's play: see pp. 42–44, 211–12.

her elegance of spirit is shown in greater relief by Charlotte's busy pragmatism, her proper dutifulness and initiative by Charlotte's desire to assume a man's role. Imoinda initiates her own death and Oroonoko follows her model; but presumably the cool world will wag on with Charlotte and Jack Stanmore and Lucy and her booby, child-husband Daniel. It is perhaps this conditioning of and commenting on each plot by the other that effects the shift in *Oroonoko* from a fictive travel account and a novella of *préciosité* to a drama of sensibility and complexity.

In preparing this edition we are grateful to the following colleagues and friends for their help: Professors Steven Bates, Albert Braunmuller, George Guffey, William James, Maynard Mack, Donald Shevlin, and James Siemon; Edna C. Davis and the staffs of the Clark and Huntington Libraries; and, especially, Frances Reed for her lively, careful assistance.

David S. Rodes
Maximillian E. Novak

University of California,
Los Angeles

OROONOKO

Quo fata trahunt, virtus secura sequetur.
Lucan

Virtus recludens immeritis mori
Caelum, negata temptat iter via.
Hor. Od. 2. lib. 3

4. *Caelum*] *Loeb; Coelum all edns.*   4. *temptat*] *Loeb; tentat all edns.*

---

1. *Quo . . . sequetur.*] "Virtue will follow fearless wherever destiny summons her" (Lucan *The Civil War* 2. 287, trans. J. D. Duff, Loeb Library).
3–4. *Virtus . . . via.*] "True worth, opening Heaven wide for those deserving not to die, essays its course by a path denied to others . . ." (Horace *Odes* 3. 2. 21–22, trans. C. E. Bennett, Loeb Library).

To His Grace, William, Duke of Devonshire, &c.,
Lord Steward of His Majesty's Household, Knight
of the Most Noble Order of the Garter, and One of
His Majesty's Most Honorable Privy Council

MY LORD,

The best part of the fortune of my last play *(The Inno-*
cent Adultery) was that it gave me an opportunity of
making myself known to Your Grace. You were pleased
to countenance the advances which I had been a great   5
while directing and aiming at you, and have since encouraged me into an industry, which, I hope, will allow
me in this play to own (which is the only way I can)
the great obligations I have to you.

I stand engaged to Mrs. Behn for the occasion of a   10
most passionate distress in my last play; and in a conscience that I had not made her a sufficient acknowledgment, I have run further into her debt for *Oroonoko,*

4. were] *Q1–3, H, C1, S;* was   9. obligations] *Q1, Q3, H, C1–*
C2.   2, S;* obligation *Q2.*

0.1–0.4 *To . . . Council.*] William Cavendish (1640–1707) succeeded
his father as fourth Earl of Devonshire in 1684. Because of his powerful support in bringing William of Orange to England he was appointed to important offices and honors and in 1694 was created Duke
of Devonshire and Marquis of Hartington. He was a noted sportsman
and patron of the arts; between 1687 and 1706 he built Chatsworth.
He was also known for his amatory life. A poem "by a lady" upon
his death praises him, "Whose awful sweetness challenged our esteem,/
Our sex's wonder and our sex's theme;/ Whose soft commanding looks
our breasts assailed;/ He came and saw and at first sight prevailed"
(DNB).
2. *last play*] *The Fatal Marriage: Or, The Innocent Adultery* was
first acted at Drury Lane in February 1694 and published that same
year.
10–13. *I . . . acknowledgment.*] In the Dedication to *The Fatal Mar-*
riage, Southerne acknowledges that he *"took the Hint of the Tragical*
part of this Play, from a Novel of Mrs. Behn's, *called [The History of*
the Nun; Or] The Fair Vow-Breaker." He then specifies that he borrowed only *"the misfortune of a Womans having innocently two Hus-*
bands, at the same time" and apologizes for having introduced *"a little*
taste of Comedy with it, not from my own Opinion, but the present
Humour of the Town" (sigs. A2r–A2v).

with a design to oblige me to be honest; and that everyone may find me out for ingratitude when I don't say   15
all that's fit for me upon that subject. She had a great
command of the stage, and I have often wondered that
she would bury her favorite hero in a novel when she
might have revived him in the scene. She thought either
that no actor could represent him, or she could not bear 20
him represented. And I believe the last when I remember what I have heard from a friend of hers, that
she always told his story more feelingly than she writ
it. Whatever happened to him at Surinam, he has
mended his condition in England. He was born here   25
under your Grace's influence, and that has carried his
fortune farther into the world than all the poetical stars
that I could have solicited for his success. It was your
opinion, my lord, that directed me to Mr. Verbruggen;
and it was his care to maintain your opinion that directed 30
the town to me, the better part of it, the people of
quality, whose favors as I am proud of, I shall always
be industrious to preserve.

My lord, I know the respect and reverence which in
this address I ought to appear in before you, who are   35
so intimate with the ancients, so general a knower of
the several species of poetry, and so just a judge in the
trials of this kind. You have an absolute power to ar-
raign and convict, but a prevailing inclination to pardon and save; and from the humanity of your temper   40
and the true knowledge of the difficulties of succeeding
this way, never aggravate or insist upon faults

Quas aut incuria fudit,
Aut humana parum cavit Natura
(Hor. *Art. Poet.*)   45

23. his] *Q1–3, H, C1–2,* the *S.*   *H, C1–2.*
24. Whatever h a p p e n e d] *Q1–*   43. *incuria*] *Q1–3, C1–2, S;* in-
2, *S;* Whatever has happened *Q3,*   turia *H.*

43–44. *Quas . . . Natura*] "which a careless hand has let drop, or
human frailty has failed to avert" (Horace, *The Art of Poetry,* ll.
352–53, trans. H. Rushton Fairclough, Loeb Library). Horace is here
arguing that poetic carelessness can be excused "when the beauties in
a poem" are significant.

to our condemnation, where they are venial, and not
against the principles of the art we pretend to. Horace,
who found it so, says,

Gratia Regum
Pieriis tentata modis.   50

The favor of great men is the poet's inheritance, and
all ages have allowed 'em to put in their claim. I only
wish that I had merit enough to prefer me to Your
Grace, that I might deserve in some measure that patronage which you are pleased to bestow on me: that I 55
were a Horace for such a Maecenas. That I could describe what I admire and tell the world what I really
think; that as you possess those infinite advantages of
nature and fortune in so eminent a degree; that as you
so far excel in the perfections of body and mind, you 60
were designed and fashioned a prince, to be the honor
of the nation and the grace and ornament of the court.
Sir, in the fulness of happiness and blessings which you
enjoy, I can only bring in my wishes for the continuance
of 'em. They shall constantly be devoted to you, with 65
all the services of,

     My Lord,
        Your Grace's most obliged, most
           thankful, and most humble servant,
               THO. SOUTHERNE   70

70. THO. SOUTHERNE] *Q1–3, H
C2*; T. Southern *C1, S*.

49–50. *Gratia . . . modis.*] "the favor of kings was sought in Pierian
strains" (Horace, *ibid.*, ll. 404–5). Here Horace refers specifically to
Pindar, Simonides, and Bacchylides, poets of Pieria, a district of North
Thessaly, and talks generally about the various affective powers of
poetry.
56. *Maecenas*] a generous patron of the arts. The original Maecenas
was a friend of Augustus and patron of Horace and Virgil.

PROLOGUE TO OROONOKO
Sent by an (unknown hand) and spoken by Mr. Powell

As when in hostile times two neighboring states
Strive by themselves and their confederates,
The war at first is made with awkward skill
And soldiers clumsily each other kill,
Till time at length their untaught fury tames   5
And into rules their heedless rage reclaims.
Then every science by degrees is made
Subservient to the man-destroying trade:
Wit, wisdom, reading, observation, art,
A well-turned head to guide a generous heart.   10
So it may prove with our contending stages,
If you will kindly but supply their wages,
Which you with ease may furnish by retrenching
Your superfluities of wine and wenching.
Who'd grudge to spare from riot and hard drinking   15
To lay it out on means to mend his thinking?
To follow such advice you should have leisure,
Since what refines your sense refines your pleasure.

stop this buffoon-ery & listen up. It'll make your life better.

0.1. TO OROONOKO] *Q1-3, H;*   0.2. and . . . Powell] *Q1-3, C1-*
om. C1-2, S.   *2, S; om. H.*

---

3. *The war*] Though the reference is general, the audience would
have thought immediately of the war in progress between England and
France.

3. *awkward skill*] In 1692 the forces of Louis XIV seemed undefeat-
able. In June of that year six thousand English and Scottish troops
were killed at the battle of Steenkirk.

11. *contending stages*] In the autumn of 1694, Thomas Betterton,
the greatest tragic actor of the Restoration, led some of the best actors
and actresses out of the United Company to form a new company
which would perform at Lincoln's Inn Fields Theatre, opening with
Congreve's *Love for Love* on 30 April 1695. The main thrust of the
Prologue suggests that the "war" between the two bodies of actors
may produce better theater than before, if the audience will support
both Companies, just as the war in Flanders has made the English
soldiers better fighters.

16. *mend*] improve.

18. *sense*] perhaps used ironically with the double meaning of
feeling and intelligence.

Women grown tame by use each fool can get,
But cuckolds all are made by men of wit.   20
To virgin favors fools have no pretense,
For maidenheads were made for men of sense. → Only Smart
'Tis not enough to have a horse well bred;   men get
To show his mettle, he must be well fed.   Sex?
Nor is it all in provender and breed;   25
He must be tried and strained to mend his speed.
A favored poet, like a pampered horse,
Will strain his eye-balls out to win the course.
Do you but in your wisdoms vote it fit
To yield due succors to this war of wit,   30
The buskin with more grace shall tread the stage,
Love sigh in softer strains, heroes less rage,
Satire shall show a triple row of teeth,
And comedy shall laugh your fops to death,
Wit shall refine, and Pegasus shall foam   35
And soar in search of ancient Greece and Rome.
And since the nation's in the conquering fit,
As you by arms, we'll vanquish France in wit.
The work were over, could our poets write
With half the spirit that our soldiers fight.   40

---

28. *course*] race.
31. *buskin*] the high boot worn by actors in ancient Athenian tragedy, often used figuratively to stand for tragedy.
33. *Satire . . . teeth*] Satire was often represented allegorically with teeth and claws to tear and a whip-like tail to sting.
35. *Pegasus*] the horse of the Muses and hence a symbol for the power of art, particularly poetry.
37. *conquering fit*] a direct reference to England's great victory over France in the taking of Namur on 5 September 1695. It was a turning point in the war for England and the Allies and led directly to the Treaty of Ryswick in 1697.

PERSONS REPRESENTED

Men

	By	
OROONOKO	*Mr. Verbruggen*	
ABOAN	*Mr. Powell*	5
LIEUTENANT GOVERNOR OF SURINAM	*Mr. Williams*	
BLANFORD	*Mr. Harland*	
STANMORE	*Mr. Horden*	
JACK STANMORE	*Mr. Mills*	
CAPTAIN DRIVER	*Mr. Ben. Johnson*	10
DANIEL, son to Widow Lackitt	*Mr. Mich. Lee*	
HOTTMAN	*Mr. Sympson*	

PLANTERS, INDIANS, NEGROES, MEN, WOMEN, AND CHILDREN.

Women

	By	15
IMOINDA	*Mrs. Rogers*	

1. PERSONS REPRESENTED]
Q1–3; Dramatis Personae *H, C1–*
2, S; precedes Dedication in Q2;
actors' names om. H.

3. By] *Q1–3; om. H, C1–2, S.*
10. Ben.] *Q1–2; B. Q3, C1–2, S.*
11. Mich.] *Q1–2; M. Q3, C1–2,*
S.

---

4. *Mr. Verbruggen*] After the defection of Betterton's players, John Verbruggen was the principal actor in Christopher Rich's Company at Drury Lane. He specialized in the roles of young lovers (Loveless in both Cibber's *Love's Last Shift* and Vanbrugh's *The Relapse*) and in heroic parts such as Oroonoko. Critick in *A Comparison between the Two Stages* (1702) complains satirically that he was "A fellow with a crackt Voice: He clangs his words as if he spoke out of a broken Drum" (ed. Staring B. Wells [Princeton, 1942], p. 106). On the other hand, Anthony Aston asserts that Verbruggen spoke the part of Oroonoko "like a Lyon" and though he was a "rough Diamond," he "shone more bright than all the artful, polish'd Brillants that ever sparkled on our Stage." In Aston's opinion, Betterton represented refined artfulness, while *"Verbruggen* was Nature, without Extravagance—Freedom, without Licentiousness—and vociferous, without bellowing," and he was capable of being "most indulgently soft" ("A Brief Supplement" to *An Apology for the Life of Mr. Colley Cibber*, ed. Robert W. Lowe [London, 1889], 2: 311–13).

16. *Mrs. Rogers*] Jane Rogers often played the role of an innocent young woman, including that of Amanda in Vanbrugh's very successful *The Relapse* (21 November 1696). In *A Comparison between the Two*

Widow Lackitt	*Mrs. Knight*
Charlotte Welldon, in man's clothes	*Mrs. Verbruggen*
Lucy Welldon, her sister	*Mrs. Lucas*

The Scene: Surinam, a colony in the West Indies, at   20
the time of the action of this tragedy in the possession
of the English.

18. clothes] *S; cloaths Q1–3, H,*   19. her   sister] *Q1–3, H, C1–2;*
C1–2.   *om. S.*

Stages (1702), however, she is called, along with Mrs. Oldfield, in
contrast to Mrs. Verbruggen, "meer Rubbish that ought to be swept off
the Stage with the Filth and Dust" (p. 106).

17. *Mrs. Knight*] Frances Knight became the principal tragic actress
at Drury Lane as well as the leading villainess after Bracegirdle, Barry,
and Leigh left to join Betterton's new company (John Harold Wilson,
All the King's Ladies [Chicago, 1958], pp. 156–59).

18. *Mrs. Verbruggen*] Susanna Percival Mountfort Verbruggen was
a celebrated comic actress particularly successful in "breeches parts."

20–22. *Surinam . . . English*] Surinam, also known as Netherlands or
Dutch Guiana, is the central area of Guiana, that northwest area of
South America bounded by the Atlantic Ocean and three rivers—the
Amazon, the Negro, and the Orinoco (from which the hero's name
may derive). By 1652 the English had substantial trading posts and
sugar-cane plantations in Surinam, and in 1663 Charles II issued letters
patent granting 120 miles of coastland to Lord Willoughby of Parham
and Lawrence Hyde. The territory was exchanged by the English for
the Dutch Colony of Nieu Amsterdam at the Treaty of Breda in 1667.

Oroonoko

ACT I

[I.i]   *Enter* Welldon *following* Lucy.

LUCY.

What will this come to? What can it end in? You have
persuaded me to leave dear England, and dearer London, the place of the world most worth living in, to
follow you a-husband-hunting into America. I thought
husbands grew in these plantations.   5

WELLDON.

Why so they do, as thick as oranges, ripening one under
another. Week after week they drop into some woman's
mouth. 'Tis but a little patience, spreading your apron
in expectation, and one of 'em will fall into your lap
at last.   10

LUCY.

Ay, so you say indeed.

WELLDON.

But you have left dear London, you say. Pray what have
you left in London that was very dear to you that had
not left you before?

LUCY.

Speak for yourself, sister.   15

WELLDON.

Nay, I'll keep you in countenance. The young fellows,
you know, the dearest part of the town and without
whom London had been a wilderness to you and me,
had forsaken us a great while.

0.1. Lucy] Lucia *Q1–3, H, C1–2,*
S; forms used indiscriminately
throughout all edns.

— 11 —

LUCY.

Forsaken us! I don't know that they ever had us.   20

WELLDON.

Forsaken us the worst way, child; that is, did not think
us worth having. They neglected us, no longer designed
upon us, they were tired of us. Women in London are
like the rich silks; they are out of fashion a great while
before they wear out—   25

LUCY.

The devil take the fashion, I say.

WELLDON.

You may tumble 'em over and over at their first coming
up and never disparage their price; but they fall upon
wearing immediately, lower and lower in their value,
till they come to the broker at last.   30

LUCY.

Ay, ay, that's the merchant they deal with. The men
would have us at their own scandalous rates. Their
plenty makes 'em wanton; and in a little time, I suppose, they won't know what they would have of the
women themselves.   35

WELLDON.

O, yes, they know what they would have. They would
have a woman give the town a pattern of her person
and beauty and not stay in it so long to have the whole
piece worn out. They would have the good face only
discovered and not the folly that commonly goes along   40
with it. They say there is a vast stock of beauty in the
nation, but a great part of it lies in unprofitable hands;
therefore for the good of the public they would have
a draft made once a quarter, send the decaying beauties
for breeders into the country to make room for new   45
faces to appear, to countenance the pleasures of the town.

LUCY.

'Tis very hard; the men must be young as long as they
live, and poor women be thought decaying and unfit
for the town at one or two and twenty. I'm sure we were
not seven years in London.   50

33. 'em] *Q1–3, H, C1–2;* them *S.*   44. draft] Draught *all edns.*

WELLDON.

Not half the time taken notice of, sister. The two or
three last years we could make nothing of it, even in
a vizard-mask; not in a vizard-mask, that has cheated
many a man into an old acquaintance. Our faces began
to be as familiar to the men of intrigue as their duns,   55
and as much avoided. We durst not appear in public
places and were almost grudged a gallery in the
churches. Even there they had their jests upon us and
cried, "She's in the right on't, good gentlewoman; since
no man considers her body, she does very well indeed   60
to take care of her soul."

LUCY.

Such unmannerly fellows there will always be.

WELLDON.

Then, you may remember, we were reduced to the last
necessity, the necessity of making silly visits to our
civil acquaintance, to bring us into tolerable company.   65
Nay, the young Inns-of-Court beaus of but one term's
standing in the fashion, who knew nobody but as they
were shown 'em by the orange-women, had nicknames
for us. How often have they laughed out, "There goes
my landlady; is not she come to let lodgings yet?"   70

LUCY.

Young coxcombs that knew no better.

WELLDON.

And that we must have come to. For your part, what
trade could you set up in? You would never arrive at

---

53. *vizard-mask*] Usually made of black velvet, this mask concealed
the entire face and ensured anonymity for its wearer. The term finally
became synonymous with "whore" in Restoration vernacular. Masks
worn in public were outlawed by Queen Anne in 1704.

55. *duns*] bill collectors.

57–58. *gallery in the churches*] The gallery or balcony of fashionable
London churches was a place to see and be seen and almost as good a
place of assignation and selection as a playhouse.

66. *young Inns-of-Court beaus*] The students at the four Inns-of-
Court, the law schools of London, were notorious for their pranks.

68. *orange-women*] sellers of oranges and fruit in the theater, justly
berated for their raucous speech and coarse manners.

the trust and credit of a guinea-bawd. You would have
too much business of your own ever to mind other 75
people's.

LUCY.

That is true indeed.

WELLDON.

Then, as a certain sign that there was nothing more to
be hoped for, the maids at the chocolate houses found
us out and laughed at us; our billet-doux lay there 80
neglected for wastepaper. We were cried down so low we
could not pass upon the city, and became so notorious
in our galloping way from one end of the town to
t'other that at last we could hardly compass a competent
change of petticoats to disguise us to the hackney coach- 85
men. And then it was near walking afoot indeed.

LUCY.

Nay, that I began to be afraid of.

WELLDON.

To prevent which, with what youth and beauty was left,
some experience, and the small remainder of fifteen
hundred pounds apiece, which amounted to bare two 90
hundred between us both, I persuaded you to bring
your person for a venture to the Indies. Everything has
succeeded in our voyage: I pass for your brother; one
of the richest planters here happening to die just as
we landed, I have claimed kindred with him; so, without 95
making his will, he has left us the credit of his rela-

74. You would] *Q1-2, C1-2, S;*
You'd *Q3, H.*

___

74. *guinea-bawd*] a female procuress. A guinea was considered the
normal sum for a professional fee; as a prefix it bore a contemptuous
connotation (*OED*).

84. *compass*] contrive, devise.

85–86. *hackney coachmen*] A hackney-coach was a four-wheeled coach,
drawn by two horses, which allowed seating for six persons and was
kept for public hire.

89–91. *small . . . both*] In the economy of later seventeenth-century
stage heiresses, several thousand pounds was considered a very attractive marriage portion. In the comic inflation of the theater Charlotte
and Lucy Welldon are clearly in desperate financial straits.

tion to trade upon. We pass for his cousins, coming here
to Surinam chiefly upon his invitation. We live in reputation, have the best acquaintance of the place; and we
shall see our account in't, I warrant you.   100

LUCY.

I must rely upon you—

Enter Widow Lackitt.

WIDOW.

Mr. Welldon, your servant. Your servant, Mrs. Lucy.
I am an ill visitor, but 'tis not too late, I hope, to bid
you welcome to this side of the world.

Salutes Lucy.

WELLDON.

Gad so, I beg your pardon, Widow, I should have done 105
the civilities of my house before; but, as you say, 'tis
not too late, I hope—   *Going to kiss her.*

WIDOW.

What! You think now this was a civil way of begging
a kiss; and by my troth, if it were, I see no harm in't;
'tis a pitiful favor indeed that is not worth asking for. 110
Though I have known a woman speak plainer before
now and not understood neither.

WELLDON.

Not under my roof. Have at you, Widow—

WIDOW.

Why, that's well said, spoke like a younger brother that
deserves to have a widow—(*He kisses her.*) You're a 115
younger brother, I know, by your kissing.

WELLDON.

How so, pray?

WIDOW.

Why, you kiss as if you expected to be paid for't. You
have birdlime upon your lips. You stick so close, there's
no getting rid of you.   120

WELLDON.

I am akin to a younger brother.

---

119. *birdlime*] a glutinous substance spread on twigs, by which birds
were caught and held fast.

WIDOW.

> So much the better. We widows are commonly the better
> for younger brothers.

LUCY.

> Better, or worse, most of you.   *(Aside.)*   But you won't
> be much better for him, I can tell you—   125

WELLDON.

> I was a younger brother; but an uncle of my mother's
> has maliciously left me an estate, and, I'm afraid, spoiled
> my fortune.

WIDOW.

> No, no, an estate will never spoil your fortune. I have
> a good estate myself, thank Heaven, and a kind hus- 130
> band that left it behind him.

WELLDON.

> Thank Heaven, that took him away from it, Widow, and
> left you behind him.

WIDOW.

> Nay, Heaven's will must be done; he's in a better place.

WELLDON.

> A better place for you, no doubt on't. Now you may 135
> look about you; choose for yourself, Mrs. Lackitt, that's
> your business; for I know you design to marry again.

WIDOW.

> O dear! Not I, I protest and swear; I don't design it.
> But I won't swear neither; one does not know what
> may happen to tempt one.   140

WELLDON.

> Why, a lusty young fellow may happen to tempt you.

WIDOW.

> Nay, I'll do nothing rashly; I'll resolve against nothing.
> The devil, they say, is very busy upon these occasions,
> especially with the widows. But if I am to be tempted,
> it must be with a young man, I promise you.—Mrs. Lucy, 145
> your brother is a very pleasant gentleman. I came about
> business to him, but he turns everything into merriment.

WELLDON.

> Business, Mrs. Lackitt? Then, I know, you would have

148. Lackitt?] Lackitt. *all edns.*

me to yourself. Pray leave us together, sister.

Exit Lucy.

(*Aside.*) What am I drawing upon myself here?   150

WIDOW.

You have taken a very pretty house here; everything so neat about you already. I hear you are laying out for a plantation.

WELLDON.

Why, yes truly, I like the country and would buy a plantation, if I could reasonably.   155

WIDOW.

O! By all means reasonably.

WELLDON.

If I could have one to my mind, I would think of settling among you.

WIDOW.

O! You can't do better. Indeed we can't pretend to have so good company for you as you had in England, but   160 we shall make very much of you. For my own part, I assure you, I shall think myself very happy to be more particularly known to you.

WELLDON.

Dear Mrs. Lackitt, you do me too much honor.

WIDOW.

Then as to a plantation, Mr. Welldon, you know I have   165 several to dispose of. Mr. Lackitt, I thank him, has left me, though I say it, the richest widow upon the place; therefore I may afford to use you better than other people can. You shall have one upon any reasonable terms.   170

WELLDON.

That's a fair offer indeed.

WIDOW.

You shall find me as easy as anybody you can have to do with, I assure you. Pray try me, I would have you try me, Mr. Welldon. Well, I like that name of yours exceedingly, Mr. Welldon.   175

167. me,] *Q1–3, H, C2; om. C1, S.*

WELLDON.

My name!

WIDOW.

O exceedingly! If anything could persuade me to alter
my own name, I verily believe nothing in the world
would do it so soon as to be called Mrs. Welldon.

WELLDON.

Why, indeed Welldon does sound something better than 180
Lackitt.

WIDOW.

O! A great deal better. Not that there is so much in a
name neither. But I don't know, there is something.
I should like mightily to be called Mrs. Welldon.

WELLDON.

I'm glad you like my name. 185

WIDOW.

Of all things. But then there's the misfortune; one can't
change one's name without changing one's condition.

WELLDON.

You'll hardly think it worth that, I believe.

WIDOW.

Think it worth what, sir? Changing my condition?
Indeed, sir, I think it worth everything. But, alas! Mr. 190
Welldon, I have been a widow but six weeks; 'tis too
soon to think of changing one's condition yet, indeed
it is. Pray don't desire it of me; not but that you may
persuade me to anything sooner than any person in the
world— 195

WELLDON.

Who, I, Mrs. Lackitt?

WIDOW.

Indeed you may, Mr. Welldon, sooner than any man
living. Lord, there's a great deal in saving a decency.
I never minded it before. Well, I'm glad you spoke first
to excuse my modesty. But what, modesty means nothing 200

189. sir?] *Q1, Q3, H,· C1–2, S;* sir, *Q2.*
191. weeks] *C1–2, S;* months *Q1–3, H.*
193. me;] me: *Q1–3, C1–2, S;* me? *H.*
196. Lackitt?] *Q1, Q3, H, C1–2, S;* Lackitt. *Q2.*

and is the virtue of a girl that does not know what she
would be at. A widow should be wiser. Now I will own
to you—but I won't confess neither—I have had a great
respect for you a great while. I beg your pardon, sir,
and I must declare to you, indeed I must, if you desire 205
to dispose of all I have in the world, in an honorable
way, which I don't pretend to be any way deserving
your consideration, my fortune and person, if you won't
understand me without telling you so, are both at your
service. Gad so! another time—   210

Stanmore *enters to 'em.*

STANMORE.

So, Mrs. Lackitt, your widowhood is waning apace. I
see which way 'tis going. Welldon, you're a happy man.
The women and their favors come home to you.

WIDOW.

A fiddle of favor, Mr. Stanmore. I am a lone woman,
you know it, left in a great deal of business, and busi- 215
ness must be followed or lost. I have several stocks and
plantations upon my hands, and other things to dispose
of, which Mr. Welldon may have occasion for.

WELLDON.

We were just upon the brink of a bargain as you came in.

STANMORE.

Let me drive it on for you.   220

WELLDON.

So you must, I believe, you or somebody for me.

STANMORE.

I'll stand by you. I understand more of this business
than you can pretend to.

WELLDON.

I don't pretend to't; 'tis quite out of my way indeed.

STANMORE.

If the widow gets you to herself, she will certainly be too 225
hard for you. I know her of old. She has no conscience

210.1 'em] *Q1–3, H, C1–2; them*   weaning *C1–2, S.*
S.   223. you] *Q1–3, H; they C1–2, S.*
211. waning] waneing *Q1–3, H;*   226. old] *Q1–3, C1–2, S; hold H.*

in a corner, a very Jew in a bargain, and would circumcise you to get more of you.

WELLDON.

Is this true, Widow?

WIDOW.

Speak as you find, Mr. Welldon; I have offered you 230 very fair. Think upon't and let me hear of you, the sooner the better, Mr. Welldon—   *Exit.*

STANMORE.

I assure you, my friend, she'll cheat you if she can.

WELLDON.

I don't know that; but I can cheat her, if I will.

STANMORE.

Cheat her? How?   235

WELLDON.

I can marry her; and then I'm sure I have it in my power to cheat her.

STANMORE.

Can you marry her?

WELLDON.

Yes, faith, so she says. Her pretty person and fortune (which, one with the other, you know, are not con- 240 temptible) are both at my service.

STANMORE.

Contemptible! Very considerable, i'gad, very desirable. Why, she's worth ten thousand pounds, man—a clear estate. No charge upon't but a boobily son. He indeed was to have half, but his father begot him and she 245 breeds him up not to know or have more than she has a mind to. And she has a mind to something else it seems.

WELLDON (*musing*).

There's a great deal to be made of this—

STANMORE.

A handsome fortune may be made on't; and I advise you 250 to't, by all means.

---

240. which, one] *Q1, Q3, H, C1–2, S;* which one, *Q2.*

247. to.] too: *Q1, Q3, H, C1–2, S;* too; *Q2.*

WELLDON.

    To marry her! An old, wanton witch! I hate her.

STANMORE.

    No matter for that. Let her go to the devil for you.
She'll cheat her son of a good estate for you. That's
a perquisite of a widow's portion always.   255

WELLDON.

    I have a design and will follow her at least till I have
a pen'worth of the plantation.

STANMORE.

    I speak as a friend when I advise you to marry her.
For 'tis directly against the interest of my own family.
My cousin Jack has belabored her a good while that way. 260

WELLDON.

    What! Honest Jack! I'll not hinder him. I'll give over
the thoughts of her.

STANMORE.

    He'll make nothing on't; she does not care for him.
I'm glad you have her in your power.

WELLDON.

    I may be able to serve him.   265

STANMORE.

    Here's a ship come into the river; I was in hopes it
had been from England.

WELLDON.

    From England!

STANMORE.

    No, I was disappointed; I long to see this handsome
cousin of yours. The picture you gave me of her has 270
charmed me.

WELLDON.

    You'll see whether it has flattered her or no in a little
time. If she recovered of that illness that was the reason
of her staying behind us, I know she will come with
the first opportunity. We shall see her, or hear of her 275
death.

273. recovered] *Q1–3, C1–2, S;*
be recovered *H.*

STANMORE.

> We'll hope the best. The ships from England are
> expected every day.

WELLDON.

> What ship is this?

STANMORE.

> A rover, a buccaneer, a trader in slaves. That's the 280
> commodity we deal in, you know. If you have a curiosity
> to see our manner of marketing, I'll wait upon you.

WELLDON.

> We'll take my sister with us.   *Exeunt.*

[I.ii]   *An open place.*
        Enter Lieutenant Governor *and* Blanford.

GOVERNOR.

> There's no resisting your fortune, Blanford; you draw
> all the prizes.

BLANFORD.

> I draw for our Lord Governor, you know; his fortune
> favors me.

GOVERNOR.

> I grudge him nothing this time; but if fortune had   5
> favored me in the last sale, the fair slave had been
> mine; Clemene had been mine.

BLANFORD.

> Are you still in love with her?

GOVERNOR.

> Every day more in love with her.

Enter Captain Driver, *teased and pulled about by* Widow Lackitt
and several Planters. *Enter at another door* Welldon, Lucy,
Stanmore [*and* Jack Stanmore].

---

280. *A rover, a buccaneer, a trader in slaves*] A *rover* was a pirate
ship; a *buccaneer* referred more specifically to a pirate ship which
raided coastal regions.

1. S.P. *Governor*] i.e., the Lieutenant Governor; so designated
throughout. The Lord Governor himself is absent (I.ii.223–26) and
never appears in the play. Blanford praises him (II.ii.20–23), but
Aboan warns Oroonoko against trust in him (III.ii.193–205).

WIDOW.

Here have I six slaves in my lot and not a man among   10
'em, all women and children; what can I do with 'em,
Captain? Pray consider, I am a woman myself and
can't get my own slaves as some of my neighbors do.

1 PLANTER.

I have all men in mine. Pray, Captain, let the men and
women be mingled together, for procreation sake, and   15
the good of the plantation.

2 PLANTER.

Ay, ay, a man and a woman, Captain, for the good of the
plantation.

CAPTAIN.

Let 'em mingle together and be damned, what care I?
Would you have me pimp for the good of the plantation?   20

1 PLANTER.

I am a constant customer, Captain.

WIDOW.

I am always ready money to you, Captain.

1 PLANTER.

For that matter, mistress, my money is as ready as yours.

WIDOW.

Pray hear me, Captain.

CAPTAIN.

Look you, I have done my part by you; I have brought   25
the number of slaves you bargained for; if your lots
have not pleased you, you must draw again among your-
selves.

3 PLANTER.

I am contented with my lot.

4 PLANTER.

I am very well satisfied.   30

14. mine] *Q1, Q1, H, C1–2, S;*
time *Q2.*

---

10. *in my lot*] In Behn's *Oroonoko,* the system of apportioning the
slaves among the planters is explained in terms of selection by lot,
"and perhaps in one Lot that may be for ten, there may happen to
be three or four Men, the rest Women and Children. Or be there
more or less of either Sex, you are obliged to be contented with your
Lot" (Behn, 5: 133).

3 PLANTER.

We'll have no drawing again.

CAPTAIN.

Do you hear, mistress? You may hold your tongue. For
my part, I expect my money.

WIDOW.

Captain, nobody questions or scruples the payment. But
I won't hold my tongue; 'tis too much to pray and pay   35
too. One may speak for one's own, I hope.

CAPTAIN.

Well, what would you say?

WIDOW.

I say no more than I can make out.

CAPTAIN.

Out with it then.

WIDOW.

I say, things have not been so fair carried as they might   40
have been. How do I know how you have juggled
together in my absence? You drew the lots before I
came, I'm sure.

CAPTAIN.

That's your own fault, mistress; you might have come
sooner.   45

WIDOW.

Then here's a prince, as they say, among the slaves, and
you set him down to go as a common man.

CAPTAIN.

Have you a mind to try what a man he is? You'll find
him no more than a common man at your business.

WIDOW.

Sir, you're a scurvy fellow to talk at this rate to me.   50
If my husband were alive, gadsbodykins, you would not
use me so.

CAPTAIN.

Right, mistress, I would not use you at all.

WIDOW.

Not use me! Your betters every inch of you, I would have

41. know how] *Q1–3, H, C1–2;*
know but *S.*

you to know, would be glad to use me, sirrah. Marry   55
come up here, who are you, I trow? You begin to think
yourself a captain, forsooth, because we call you so.
You forget yourself as fast as you can, but I remember
you; I know you for a pitiful, paltry fellow, as you are,
an upstart to prosperity, one that is but just come   60
acquainted with cleanliness and that never saw five
shillings of your own without deserving to be hanged
for 'em.

GOVERNOR.

She has given you a broadside, Captain. You'll stand up
to her.   65

CAPTAIN.

Hang her, stink-pot, I'll come no nearer.

WIDOW.

By this good light, it would make a woman do a thing
she never designed: marry again, though she were sure
to repent it, to be revenged of such a—

JACK STANMORE.

What's the matter, Mrs. Lackitt? Can I serve you?   70

WIDOW.

No, no, you can't serve me. You are for serving yourself,
I'm sure. Pray go about your business, I have none for
you. You know I have told you so. Lord! How can you
be so troublesome? Nay, so unconscionable to think that
every rich widow must throw herself away upon a young   75
fellow that has nothing?

STANMORE.

Jack, you are answered, I suppose.

JACK STANMORE.

I'll have another pluck at her.

WIDOW.

Mr. Welldon, I am a little out of order, but pray bring
your sister to dine with me. Gad's my life, I'm out of   80

66. nearer] *Q2, C1–2, S;* near
Q1, Q3, H.

---

64. *broadside*] the simultaneous discharge of all the artillery from
one side of a ship of war (*OED*).

all patience with that pitiful fellow. My flesh rises at him.
I can't stay in the place where he is—   *Exit.*

BLANFORD.

Captain, you have used the widow very familiarly.

CAPTAIN.

This is my way; I have no design and therefore am not
over-civil. If she had ever a handsome daughter to   85
wheedle her out of, or if I could make anything of her
booby son—

WELLDON (*aside*).

I may improve that hint and make something of him.

GOVERNOR.

She's very rich.

CAPTAIN.

I'm rich myself. She has nothing that I want. I have no   90
leaks to stop. Old women are fortune-menders. I have
made a good voyage and would reap the fruits of my
labor. We plow the deep, my masters, but our harvest is
on shore. I'm for a young woman.

STANMORE.

Look about, Captain, there's one ripe and ready for the   95
sickle.

CAPTAIN.

A woman indeed! I will be acquainted with her. Who
is she?

WELLDON.

My sister, sir.

CAPTAIN.

Would I were akin to her. If she were my sister, she   100
should never go out of the family. What say you, mistress? You expect I should marry you, I suppose.

LUCY.

I shan't be disappointed if you don't.   *Turning away.*

WELLDON.

She won't break her heart, sir.

CAPTAIN.

But I mean—   *Following her.*   105

WELLDON.

And I mean—(*going between him and* Lucy) that you
must not think of her without marrying.

CAPTAIN.

I mean so too.

WELLDON.

Why then your meaning's out.

CAPTAIN.

You're very short.   110

WELLDON.

I will grow and be taller for you.

CAPTAIN.

I shall grow angry and swear.

WELLDON.

You'll catch no fish then.

CAPTAIN.

I don't well know whether he designs to affront me or
no.   115

STANMORE.

No, no, he's a little familiar; 'tis his way.

CAPTAIN.

Say you so? Nay, I can be as familiar as he, if that be it.
Well, sir, look upon me full. What say you? How do
you like me for a brother-in-law?

WELLDON.

Why yes, faith, you'll do my business (*turning him* 120
about), if we can agree about my sister's.

CAPTAIN.

I don't know whether your sister will like me or not.
I can't say much to her. But I have money enough; and
if you are her brother, as you seem to be akin to her,
I know that will recommend me to you.   125

WELLDON.

This is your market for slaves; my sister is a free woman
and must not be disposed of in public. You shall be
welcome to my house, if you please. And upon better
acquaintance, if my sister likes you, and I like your
offers—   130

CAPTAIN.

Very well, sir, I'll come and see her.

---

113. *You'll . . . then*] "If you swear, you'll catch no Fish" is an old
proverb, now out of use (Tilley, F 315).

GOVERNOR.

Where are the slaves, Captain? They are long a-coming.

BLANFORD.

And who is this prince that's fallen to my lot for the
Lord Governor? Let me know something of him that I
may treat him accordingly; who is he?   135

CAPTAIN.

He's the devil of a fellow. I can tell you—a prince
every inch of him. You have paid dear enough for him
for all the good he'll do you. I was forced to clap him
in irons and did not think the ship safe neither. You
are in hostility with the Indians, they say; they threaten   140
you daily. You had best have an eye upon him.

BLANFORD.

But who is he?

GOVERNOR.

And how do you know him to be a prince?

CAPTAIN.

He is son and heir to the great King of Angola, a mis-
chievous monarch in those parts, who by his good will   145
would never let any of his neighbors be in quiet. This
son was his general, a plaguy fighting fellow. I have
formerly had dealings with him for slaves which he took
prisoners, and have got pretty roundly by him. But the
wars being at an end and nothing more to be got by   150
the trade of that country, I made bold to bring the
prince along with me.

GOVERNOR.

How could you do that?

BLANFORD.

What! Steal a prince out of his own country? Impossible!

CAPTAIN.

'Twas hard indeed, but I did it. You must know, this   155
Oroonoko—

---

144. *Angola*] A Portuguese corruption of the Bantu *Ngola*, the name
of an area in West Africa south of the equator owned (until 1975) by
Portugal. In Behn, Oroonoko is from "Coramantien." For some possible reasons for this change, see Introduction, above, p. xxxvii, n. 73.
   147. *plaguy*] troublesome.

BLANFORD.

Is that his name?

CAPTAIN.

Ay, Oroonoko.

GOVERNOR.

Oroonoko—

CAPTAIN.

Is naturally inquisitive about the men and manners of 160
the white nations. Because I could give him some
account of the other parts of the world, I grew very
much into his favor. In return of so great an honor, you
know I could do no less upon my coming away than
invite him on board me. Never having been in a ship, he 165
appointed his time and I prepared my entertainment.
He came the next evening as privately as he could, with
about some twenty along with him. The punch went
round, and as many of his attendants as would be dangerous I sent dead drunk on shore; the rest we secured. 170
And so you have the Prince Oroonoko.

1 PLANTER.

Gad-a-mercy, Captain, there you were with him, i'faith.

2 PLANTER.

Such men as you are fit to be employed in public
affairs. The plantation will thrive by you.

3 PLANTER.

Industry should be encouraged.   175

CAPTAIN.

There's nothing done without it, boys. I have made my
fortune this way.

BLANFORD.

Unheard-of villainy!

STANMORE.

Barbarous treachery!

BLANFORD.

They applaud him for't.   180

GOVERNOR.

But, Captain, methinks you have taken a great deal of

159. Oroonoko—] Oroonoko. *all*
edns.

— 29 —

pains for this Prince Oroonoko; why did you part with
him at the common rate of slaves?

CAPTAIN.

Why, Lieutenant Governor, I'll tell you; I did design to
carry him to England to have showed him there, but I 185
found him troublesome upon my hands and I'm glad I'm
rid of him.- —O, ho, here they come.

*Black slaves, men, women, and children, pass across the stage by
two and two;* Aboan, *and others of Oroonoko's attendants two
and two;* Oroonoko *last of all in chains.*

LUCY.

Are all these wretches slaves?

STANMORE.

All sold, they and their posterity all slaves.

LUCY.

O miserable fortune!   190

BLANFORD.

Most of 'em know no better; they were born so and only
change their masters. But a prince, born only to command, betrayed and sold! My heart drops blood for him.

CAPTAIN.

Now, Governor, here he comes, pray observe him.

OROONOKO.

So, sir, you have kept your word with me.   195

CAPTAIN.

I am a better Christian, I thank you, than to keep it
with a heathen.

OROONOKO.

You are a Christian, be a Christian still.
If you have any god that teaches you
To break your word, I need not curse you more.   200
Let him cheat you, as you are false to me.

187. here] *Q1–2;* heark *Q3, H,*   191. better;] *Q1–2;* better! *Q3,*
C1–2, S.   *H, C1–2, S.*

195. *So, sir . . .*] Oroonoko's iambic pentameter is a dramatic device,
the sign of the heroic personage. As the noble protagonist of this
drama, he not only speaks exclusively in heroic verse, but inspires
those around him to a like pattern.

You faithful followers of my better fortune!
We have been fellow-soldiers in the field;

Embracing his friends.

Now we are fellow-slaves. This last farewell.
Be sure of one thing that will comfort us: 205
Whatever world we next are thrown upon
Cannot be worse than this.

All slaves go off but Oroonoko.

CAPTAIN.

You see what a bloody pagan he is, Governor; but I took
care that none of his followers should be in the same
lot with him for fear they should undertake some 210
desperate action to the danger of the colony.

OROONOKO.

Live still in fear; it is the villain's curse
And will revenge my chains. Fear even me
Who have no pow'r to hurt thee. Nature abhors
And drives thee out from the society   215
And commerce of mankind for breach of faith.
Men live and prosper but in mutual trust,
A confidence of one another's truth.
That thou hast violated. I have done.
I know my fortune and submit to it.   220

GOVERNOR.

Sir, I am sorry for your fortune and would help it if I
could.

BLANFORD.

Take off his chains. You know your condition, but you
are fallen into honorable hands. You are the Lord
Governor's slave, who will use you nobly. In his absence 225
it shall be my care to serve you.

Blanford applying to him.

OROONOKO.

I hear you, but I can believe no more.

GOVERNOR.

Captain, I'm afraid the world won't speak so honor-
ably of this action of yours as you would have 'em.

221. Sir.] *Q1, Q3, H, C1–2, S;*
om. Q2.

CAPTAIN.

    I have the money. Let the world speak and be damned; 230
    I care not.

OROONOKO.

    I would forget myself.

                     (*To* Blanford.) Be satisfied,
    I am above the rank of common slaves.
    Let that content you. The Christian there that knows me,
    For his own sake will not discover more.   235

CAPTAIN.

    I have other matters to mind. You have him, and much
    good may do you with your prince.   *Exit.*

       The Planters *pulling and staring at* Oroonoko.

BLANFORD.

    What would you have there? You stare as if you never
    saw a man before. Stand further off.   *Turns 'em away.*

OROONOKO.

    Let 'em stare on.   240
    I am unfortunate, but not ashamed
    Of being so. No, let the guilty blush,
    The white man that betrayed me. Honest black
    Disdains to change its color. I am ready.
    Where must I go? Dispose me as you please.   245
    I am not well acquainted with my fortune,
    But must learn to know it better; so I know, you say:
    Degrees make all things easy.

BLANFORD.

    All things shall be easy.

OROONOKO.

    Tear off this pomp and let me know myself.   250
    The slavish habit best becomes me now.
    Hard fare and whips and chains may overpow'r
    The frailer flesh and bow my body down.
    But there's another, nobler part of me,
    Out of your reach, which you can never tame.   255

247. better;] better: *Q1, Q3, H,*   247. say:] *Q1–3, H, C1–2;* say, *S.*
C1–2, S; better. *Q2.*

BLANFORD.

You shall find nothing of this wretchedness
You apprehend. We are not monsters all.
You seem unwilling to disclose yourself;
Therefore, for fear the mentioning your name
Should give you new disquiets, I presume   260
To call you Caesar.

OROONOKO.

I am myself, but call me what you please.

STANMORE.

A very good name, Caesar.

GOVERNOR.

And very fit for his great character.

OROONOKO.

Was Caesar then a slave?   265

GOVERNOR.

I think he was, to pirates too. He was a great conqueror,
but unfortunate in his friends—

OROONOKO.

His friends were Christians?

BLANFORD.

No.

OROONOKO.

No! That's strange.   270

GOVERNOR.

And murdered by 'em.

OROONOKO.

I would be Caesar then. Yet I will live.

BLANFORD.

Live to be happier.

259. Therefore.] *C1–2, S;* There- | 272. then.] *The British Theatre,*
fore *Q1–3, H.* | ed. Inchbald, 7 (London, 1808):
264. great] *Q1–3, C1–2; om. H,* | 15; there. *Q1, Q3, H, C1–2, S;*
S. | there; *Q2.*

265–66. *Caesar . . . to pirates*] According to legend, Julius Caesar was
captured by Mediterranean pirates, who were amused by his boldness
and his threat to have them crucified. Regaining his freedom, he, in
turn, captured the pirates, recovered his ransom, and made good his
threat. See *The Oxford Companion to Classical Literature,* ed. Sir
Paul Harvey (Oxford, 1962), p. 84.

OROONOKO.

Do what you will with me.

BLANFORD.

I'll wait upon you, attend, and serve you.   275

Exit with Oroonoko.

LUCY.

Well, if the Captain had brought this prince's country
along with him and would make me queen of it, I would
not have him after doing so base a thing.

WELLDON.

He's a man to thrive in the world, sister. He'll make
you the better jointure.   280

LUCY.

Hang him, nothing can prosper with him.

STANMORE.

Enquire into the great estates, and you will find most
of 'em depend upon the same title of honesty. The men
who raise 'em first are much of the Captain's principles.

WELLDON.

Ay, ay, as you say, let him be damned for the good of 285
his family. Come, sister, we are invited to dinner.

GOVERNOR.

Stanmore, you dine with me.   *Exeunt omnes.*

ACT II

[II.i]   *Widow Lackitt's house.*
    Enter Widow Lackitt, Welldon.

WELLDON.

This is so great a favor I don't know how to receive it.

WIDOW.

O dear sir! You know how to receive and how to return
a favor as well as anybody, I don't doubt it. 'Tis not
the first you have had from our sex, I suppose.

WELLDON.

But this is so unexpected.   5

WIDOW.

Lord, how can you say so, Mr. Welldon? I won't believe
you. Don't I know you handsome gentlemen expect
everything that a woman can do for you? And by my
troth you're in the right on't. I think one can't do too
much for a handsome gentleman, and so you shall find it.   10

WELLDON.

I shall never have such an offer again, that's certain.
What shall I do? I am mightily divided.

                                    Pretending a concern.

WIDOW.

Divided! O dear, I hope not so, sir. If I marry, truly I
expect to have you to myself.

WELLDON.

There's no danger of that, Mrs. Lackitt. I am divided   15
in my thoughts. My father upon his death bed obliged
me to see my sister disposed of before I married myself.
'Tis that sticks upon me. They say indeed promises are
to be broken or kept, and I know 'tis a foolish thing to
be tied to a promise, but I can't help it. I don't know   20
how to get rid of it.

WIDOW.

Is that all?

WELLDON.

All in all to me. The commands of a dying father, you
know, ought to obeyed.

WIDOW.

And so they may. 25

WELLDON.

Impossible, to do me any good.

WIDOW.

They shan't be your hindrance. You would have a husband for your sister, you say. He must be very well to
pass too in the world, I suppose?

WELLDON.

I would not throw her away. 30

WIDOW.

Then marry her out of hand to the sea captain you were
speaking of.

WELLDON.

I was thinking of him, but 'tis to no purpose. She hates
him.

WIDOW.

Does she hate him? Nay, 'tis no matter, an impudent 35
rascal as he is, I would not advise her to marry him.

WELLDON.

Can you think of nobody else?

WIDOW.

Let me see.

WELLDON.

Ay, pray do. I should be loth to part with my good
fortune in you for so small a matter as a sister. But you 40
find how it is with me.

WIDOW.

Well remembered, i'faith. Well, if I thought you would
like of it, I have a husband for her. What do you think
of my son?

WELLDON.

You don't think of it yourself. 45

WIDOW.

I protest but I do. I am in earnest, if you are. He shall
marry her within this half hour, if you'll give your consent to it.

— 36 —

WELLDON.

I give my consent! I'll answer for my sister; she shall have him. You may be sure I shall be glad to get over 50 the difficulty.

WIDOW.

No more to be said then; that difficulty is over. But I vow and swear you frightened me, Mr. Welldon. If I had not had a son now for your sister, what must I have done, do you think? Were not you an ill-natured 55 thing to boggle at a promise? I could break twenty for you.

WELLDON.

I am the more obliged to you. But this son will save all.

WIDOW.

He's in the house; I'll go and bring him myself. *(Going.)* You would do well to break the business to your sister. 60 She's within; I'll send her to you— *Going again, comes back.*

WELLDON.

Pray do.

WIDOW.

But d'you hear? Perhaps she may stand upon her maidenly behavior and blush and play the fool and delay. But don't be answered so. What! She is not a 65 girl at these years; show your authority and tell her roundly she must be married immediately. I'll manage my son, I warrant you. *Goes out in haste.*

WELLDON.

The widow's in haste, I see. I thought I had laid a rub in the road about my sister, but she has stepped over 70 that. She's making way for herself as fast as she can, but little thinks where she is going. I could tell her she is going to play the fool, but people don't love to hear of their faults. Besides, that is not my business at present.

Enter Lucy.

So, sister, I have a husband for you— 75

LUCY.

With all my heart. I don't know what confinement marriage may be to the men, but I'm sure the women have no liberty without it. I am for anything that will deliver

me from the care of a reputation, which I begin to find
impossible to preserve. 80

WELLDON.

I'll ease you of that care. You must be married immediately.

LUCY.

The sooner the better, for I am quite tired of setting
up for a husband. The widow's foolish son is the man,
I suppose. 85

WELLDON.

I considered your constitution, sister, and finding you
would have occasion for a fool, I have provided accordingly.

LUCY.

I don't know what occasion I may have for a fool when
I'm married, but I find none but fools have occasion to 90
marry.

WELLDON.

Since he is to be a fool then, I thought it better for you
to have one of his mother's making than your own; 'twill
save you the trouble.

LUCY.

I thank you; you take a great deal of pains for me. But, 95
pray tell me, what are you doing for yourself all this
while?

WELLDON.

You were never true to your own secrets, and therefore
I won't trust you with mine. Only remember this, I am
your elder sister, and consequently laying my breeches 100
aside, have as much occasion for a husband as you can
have. I have a man in my eye, be satisfied.

Enter Widow Lackitt, *with her son* Daniel.

WIDOW.

Come, Daniel, hold up thy head, child. Look like a
man. You must not take it as you have done. Gad's my

97. while?] *Q1, Q3, H, C1–2,*
S; while. *Q2.*

life! There's nothing to be done with twirling your 105
hat, man.

DANIEL.

Why, mother, what's to be done then?

WIDOW.

Why look me in the face and mind what I say to you.

DANIEL.

Marry, who's the fool then? What shall I get by mind-
ing what you say to me?   110

WIDOW.

Mrs. Lucy, the boy is bashful; don't discourage him.
Pray come a little forward and let him salute you.

> *Going between* Lucy *and* Daniel.

LUCY *(to* Welldon).

A fine husband I am to have truly.

WIDOW.

Come, Daniel, you must be acquainted with this gentlewoman.   115

DANIEL.

Nay, I'm not proud, that is not my fault. I am presently
acquainted when I know the company, but this gentlewoman is a stranger to me.

WIDOW.

She is your mistress. I have spoke a good word for you;
make her a bow and go and kiss her.   120

DANIEL.

Kiss her! Have a care what you say; I warrant she
scorns your words. Such fine folk are not used to be
slopped and kissed. Do you think I don't know that,
mother?

WIDOW.

Try her, try her, man.   125

> Daniel *bows. She thrusts him forward.*

Why, that's well done; go nearer her.

---

107. then?] *Q1, Q3, H, C1–2,*   126. Why,] *Q2;* Why *Q1, Q3, H,*
S; then, *Q2.*   *C1–2, S.*
111. him.] him: *Q1, Q3, H, C1–*
2, S; him; *Q2.*

DANIEL (*to his mother*).

> Is the devil in the woman? Why, so I can go nearer her,
> if you would let a body alone. (*To* Lucy.) Cry you
> mercy, forsooth; my mother is always shaming one
> before company. She would have me as unmannerly as 130
> herself and offer to kiss you.

WELLDON.

> Why, won't you kiss her?

DANIEL.

> Why, pray, may I?

WELLDON.

> Kiss her, kiss her, man.

DANIEL.

> Marry, and I will. (*Kisses her.*) Gadzooks! She kisses 135
> rarely! An' please you, mistress, and seeing my mother
> will have it so, I don't much care if I kiss you again,
> forsooth.   *Kisses her again.*

LUCY.

> Well, how do you like me now?

DANIEL.

> Like you! Marry, I don't know. You have bewitched me, 140
> I think. I was never so in my born days before.

WIDOW.

> You must marry this fine woman, Daniel.

DANIEL.

> Hey day! Marry her! I was never married in all my life.
> What must I do with her then, mother?

WIDOW.

> You must live with her, eat and drink with her, go to bed 145
> with her, and sleep with her.

DANIEL.

> Nay, marry, if I must go to bed with her, I shall never
> sleep, that's certain. She'll break me of my rest quite
> and clean, I tell you beforehand. As for eating and
> drinking with her, why I have a good stomach and can 150
> play my part in any company. But how do you think I
> can go to bed to a woman I don't know?

127. Why,] *Q2;* Why *Q1, Q3, H,*   139. now?] *Q1, Q3, H, S;* now.
C1–2, S.   *Q2;* now! *C1–2.*

WELLDON.

You shall know her better.

DANIEL.

Say you so, sir?

WELLDON.

Kiss her again.   Daniel *kisses* Lucy. 155

DANIEL.

Nay, kissing I find will make us presently acquainted.
We'll steal into a corner to practice a little, and then I
shall be able to do anything.

WELLDON.

The young man mends apace.

WIDOW.

Pray don't balk him.   160

DANIEL.

Mother, mother, if you'll stay in the room by me and
promise not to leave me, I don't care for once if I
venture to go to bed with her.

WIDOW.

There's a good child. Go in and put on thy best clothes.
Pluck up a spirit; I'll stay in the room by thee. She won't 165
hurt thee, I warrant thee.

DANIEL.

Nay, as to that matter, I'm not afraid of her. I'll give
her as good as she brings. I have a Roland for her
Oliver, and so you may tell her.   *Exit.*

WIDOW.

Mrs. Lucy, we shan't stay for you. You are in a readi- 170
ness, I suppose.

WELLDON.

She's always ready to do what I would have her, I must
say that for my sister.

WIDOW.

'Twill be her own another day. Mr. Welldon, we'll marry
'em out of hand, and then—   175

___

168–69. *Roland . . . Oliver*] The reference is to the hero and his
priest-adviser in the medieval French epic *The Song of Roland*, who
were "brave" and "wise" respectively; a variation (Tilley, R 195) of
the proverbial "tit for tat" (T 356), with a distinct sexual innuendo,
based on "roll" and "O."

WELLDON.

 And then, Mrs. Lackitt, look to yourself.   *Exuent.*

[II.ii]   *[Enter]* Oroonoko *and* Blanford.

OROONOKO.

 You grant I have good reason to suspect
 All the professions you can make to me.

BLANFORD.

 Indeed you have.

OROONOKO.

 The dog that sold me did profess as much
 As you can do—but yet I know not why—   5
 Whether it is because I'm fall'n so low
 And have no more to fear—that is not it:
 I am a slave no longer than I please.
 'Tis something nobler: being just myself,
 I am inclining to think others so.   10
 'Tis that prevails upon me to believe you.

BLANFORD.

 You may believe me.

OROONOKO.   I do believe you.
 From what I know of you, you are no fool.
 Fools only are the knaves and live by tricks;
 Wise men may thrive without 'em and be honest.   15

BLANFORD *(aside).*

 They won't all take your counsel—

OROONOKO.

 You know my story and you say you are
 A friend to my misfortunes. That's a name
 Will teach you what you owe yourself and me.

BLANFORD.

 I'll study to deserve to be your friend.   20
 When once our noble governor arrives,
 With him you will not need my interest;
 He is too generous not to feel your wrongs.

---

 14. *Fools . . . knaves*] the familiar division of all mankind during
the Restoration into those who do (*knaves*) and the rest who are done
to (*fools*).

But be assured I will employ my pow'r
And find the means to send you home again.   25

OROONOKO.

I thank you, sir—(*sighing*) my honest, wretched friends!
Their chains are heavy. They have hardly found
So kind a master. May I ask you, sir,
What is become of 'em? Perhaps I should not.
You will forgive a stranger.

BLANFORD.   I'll enquire,   30
And use my best endeavors, where they are,
To have 'em gently used.

OROONOKO.   Once more I thank you.
You offer every cordial that can keep
My hopes alive to wait a better day.
What friendly care can do, you have applied.   35
But, O! I have a grief admits no cure.

BLANFORD.

You do not know, sir—

OROONOKO.   Can you raise the dead?
Pursue and overtake the wings of time?
And bring about again the hours, the days,
The years that made me happy?   40

BLANFORD.

That is not to be done.

OROONOKO.

No, there is nothing to be done for me.
                              Kneeling and kissing the earth.
Thou god-adored! Thou ever-glorious sun!
If she be yet on earth, send me a beam
Of thy all-seeing power to light me to her,   45
Or if thy sister goddess has preferred
Her beauty to the skies to be a star,
O tell me where she shines, that I may stand
Whole nights and gaze upon her.

BLANFORD.

I am rude and interrupt you.

40. happy?] *C1–2; happy. Q1–3,
H, S.*

OROONOKO.   I am troublesome.   50
    But pray give me your pardon. My swoll'n heart
    Bursts out its passage, and I must complain.
    O! Can you think of nothing dearer to me—
    Dearer than liberty, my country, friends,
    Much dearer than my life—that I have lost: 55
    The tend'rest, best belov'd, and loving wife.

BLANFORD.
    Alas! I pity you.
OROONOKO.   Do, pity me.
    Pity's akin to love, and every thought
    Of that soft kind is welcome to my soul.
    I would be pitied here.
BLANFORD.   I dare not ask   60
    More than you please to tell me, but if you
    Think it convenient to let me know
    Your story, I dare promise you to bear
    A part in your distress, if not assist you.
OROONOKO.
    Thou honest-hearted man! I wanted such,   65
    Just such a friend as thou art, that would sit
    Still as the night and let me talk whole days
    Of my Imoinda. O! I'll tell thee all
    From first to last, and pray observe me well.
BLANFORD.
    I will most heedfully.   70
OROONOKO.
    There was a stranger in my father's court
    Valued and honored much. He was a white,
    The first I ever saw of your complexion.
    He changed his gods for ours and so grew great;
    Of many virtues and so famed in arms   75
    He still commanded all my father's wars.
    I was bred under him. One fatal day,
    The armies joining, he before me stepped,
    Receiving in his breast a poisoned dart

53. me—] *all edns.*

---

76. *still*] ever.

Levelled at me; he died within my arms.   80
I've tired you already.
BLANFORD.   Pray go on.
OROONOKO.

He left an only daughter, whom he brought
An infant to Angola. When I came
Back to the court a happy conqueror,
Humanity obliged me to condole   85
With this sad virgin for a father's loss,
Lost for my safety. I presented her
With all the slaves of battle to atone
Her father's ghost. But when I saw her face
And heard her speak, I offered up myself   90
To be the sacrifice. She bowed and blushed;
I wondered and adored. The sacred pow'r
That had subdued me then inspired my tongue,
Inclined her heart; and all our talk was love.
BLANFORD.

Then you were happy.
OROONOKO.   O! I was too happy.   95
I married her. And though my country's custom
Indulged the privilege of many wives,
I swore myself never to know but her.
She grew with child, and I grew happier still.
O my Imoinda! But it could not last.   100
Her fatal beauty reached my father's ears.
He sent for her to court, where, cursed court!
No woman comes but for his amorous use.
He raging to possess her, she was forced
To own herself my wife. The furious king   105
Started at incest. But grown desperate,

---

83. *An infant to Angola*] For discussion of Southerne's change of
Behn's "Black Venus" (5: 137, 171–72) to a white woman, see Introduction, p. xxxvii, n. 73.

96. *I married her*] Behn's account is *précieuse* but rather less sentimental about sex, love, and marriage than this. Her hero marries
Imoinda only after he has ravished her in his father's seraglio, and
the relationship between the lovers does not exclude the possibility
that Oroonoko might later drift towards polygamy—the "natural"
practice of his society. See V.v.200, and Behn, 5: 138–39, 152, 174, 202.

Not daring to enjoy what he desired,
In mad revenge, which I could never learn,
He poisoned her, or sent her far, far off,
Far from my hopes ever to see her more.   110

BLANFORD.

Most barbarous of fathers! The sad tale
Has struck me dumb with wonder.

OROONOKO.   I have done.
I'll trouble you no farther. Now and then
A sigh will have its way; that shall be all.

Enter Stanmore.

STANMORE.

Blanford, the Lieutenant Governor is gone to your plan- 115
tation. He desires you would bring the royal slave with
you. The sight of his fair mistress, he says, is an entertainment for a prince; he would have his opinion of her.

OROONOKO.

Is he a lover?

BLANFORD.

So he says himself; he flatters a beautiful slave that I 120
have and calls her mistress.

OROONOKO.

Must he then flatter her to call her mistress?
I pity the proud man who thinks himself
Above being in love. What though she be a slave,
She may deserve him.   125

BLANFORD.

You shall judge of that when you see her, sir.

OROONOKO.

I go with you.   *Exeunt.*

[II.iii]

A plantation. [*Enter*] Lieutenant Governor *following* Imoinda.

GOVERNOR.

I have disturbed you. I confess my fault,

124. What] What, *all edns.*

— 46 —

My fair Clemene, but begin again,
And I will listen to your mournful song,
Sweet as the soft complaining nightingale's.
While every note calls out my trembling soul   5
And leaves me silent as the midnight groves
Only to shelter you, sing, sing again,
And let me wonder at the many ways
You have to ravish me.

IMOINDA.   O! I can weep
Enough for you and me, if that will please you.   10

GOVERNOR.
You must not weep. I come to dry your tears
And raise you from your sorrow. Look upon me.
Look with the eyes of kind indulging love
That I may have full cause for what I say:
I come to offer you your liberty   15
And be myself the slave. You turn away.   *Following her.*
But everything becomes you. I may take
This pretty hand; I know your modesty
Would draw it back. But you would take it ill
If I should let it go, I know you would.   20
You shall be gently forced to please yourself;
That you will thank me for.

> *She struggles and gets her hand from him,*
> *then he offers to kiss her.*

Nay if you struggle with me, I must take—

IMOINDA.
You may, my life, that I can part with freely.   *Exit.*

> *Enter* Blanford, Stanmore, Oroonoko *to him.*

BLANFORD.
So, Governor, we don't disturb you, I hope. Your mistress   25
has left you. You were making love; she's thankful for
the honor, I suppose.

GOVERNOR.
Quite insensible to all I say and do.
When I speak to her, she sighs or weeps,
But never answers me as I would have her.   30

STANMORE.

There's something nearer than her slavery that touches
her.

BLANFORD.

What do her fellow slaves say of her? Can't they find
the cause?

GOVERNOR. *He's so creepy*

Some of 'em, who pretend to be wiser than the rest and 35
hate her, I suppose, for being used better than they
are, will needs have it that she's with child.

BLANFORD.

Poor wretch! If it be so, I pity her.
She has lost a husband that perhaps was dear
To her, and then you cannot blame her.   40

OROONOKO (*sighing*).

If it be so, indeed you cannot blame her.

GOVERNOR.

No, no, it is not so. If it be so,   *no*
I still must love her, and desiring still,
I must enjoy her.

BLANFORD.

Try what you can do with fair means, and welcome.   45

GOVERNOR.

I'll give you ten slaves for her.

BLANFORD.

You know she is our Lord Governor's, but if I could
dispose of her, I would not now, especially to you.

GOVERNOR.

Why not to me?

BLANFORD. *noble guy*

I mean against her will. You are in love with her, 50
And we all know what your desires would have.
Love stops at nothing but possession.
Were she within your pow'r, you do not know   *progressive*
How soon you would be tempted to forget
The nature of the deed and, maybe, act   55
A violence you after would repent.

33. her?] *Q1–3, H;* her; *C1–2, S.*   40. and] *Q1, Q3, H, C1–2, S;*
35. 'em] *Q1–3, H, C1–2;* them *S.*   *om. Q2.*

— 48 —

OROONOKO.

    'Tis godlike in you to protect the weak.

GOVERNOR.

    Fie, fie, I would not force her. Though she be

    A slave, her mind is free and should consent.

OROONOKO.

    Such honor will engage her to consent;   60

    And then, if you're in love, she's worth the having.

    Shall we not see this wonder?

GOVERNOR.   Have a care;

    You have a heart, and she has conquering eyes.

OROONOKO.

    I have a heart; but if it could be false

    To my first vows ever to love again,   65

    These honest hands should tear it from my breast

    And throw the traitor from me. O! Imoinda!

    Living or dead, I can be only thine.

BLANFORD (*to the* Governor *and* Stanmore).

    Imoinda was his wife. She's either dead

    Or living, dead to him: forced from his arms   70

    By an inhuman father. Another time

    I'll tell you all.

STANMORE.   Hark! The slaves have done their work,

    And now begins their evening merriment.

BLANFORD.

    The men are all in love with fair Clemene

    As much as you are, and the women hate her   75

    From an instinct of natural jealousy.

    They sing and dance and try their little tricks

    To entertain her and divert her sadness.

    Maybe she is among 'em. Shall we see?   *Exeunt.*

*The scene drawn shows the slaves, men, women, and children
upon the ground; some rise and dance, others sing the following
songs.*

62. care;] *Q1, Q3, H, C1–2, S;* 63. and] *Q1–3, C1–2, S;* end *H.*
care? *Q2.*

A SONG. By Sir Harry Sheers.
Set by Mr. Courtevill, and sung by the Boy to Miss Cross.

I

A lass there lives upon the green,   80
     Could I her picture draw;
A brighter nymph was never seen,
That looks and reigns a little queen
     And keeps the swains in awe.

II

Her eyes are Cupid's darts and wings,   85
     Her eyebrows are his bow,
Her silken hair the silver strings,
Which sure and swift destruction brings
     To all the vale below.

III

If Pastorella's dawning light   90
     Can warm and wound us so,
Her noon will shine so piercing bright

79.4. By . . . Sheers] *C1–2, S;* By an unknown hand *Q1–3, H.*

88. Which] *all edns.;* that *Deliciae Musicae (DM), The Fourth Book* (London, 1696).

79.4—94. *A Song . . . subdue*] This song and the following one were first printed, with music, in *Deliciae Musicae (DM), The Fourth* Book (London, 1696). They are immediately followed there by a third song, "Celemene, pray tell me," which was perhaps introduced at this point in the play (see Appendix A). The author of the lyrics of "A lass" was Sir Henry Sheeres (d. 1710), a military engineer, member of the Royal Society, and one-time friend of Pepys. According to the *DNB,* "a poem of his was prefixed to Southern's 'Oroonoko,' 1696," and the first collected edition, 1713 (Cl), of *Oroonoko* attributes these lyrics to a "Sir *Harry Sheers.*"

79.5. *Mr. Courtevill*] Ralph or Raphael Courtevill[e] (d. 1735) was an organist and composer who also wrote songs for Durfey's *Don Quixote,* Part 3, and for Dryden's *Aureng-Zebe.*

79.5. *the Boy*] probably Jemmy Bowen who was a child singer in Rich's Company at Drury Lane.

79.5. *Miss Cross*] Letitia Cross was a member of Rich's Company and one of Purcell's favorite singers. Purcell wrote many songs suited to her youth and voice; she was probably about sixteen when she first sang in *Oroonoko.* See Appendix A.

Each glancing beam will kill outright
And every swain subdue.

A SONG. By Mr. Cheek.
Set by Mr. Courtevill, and sung by Mr. Leveridge.

I

Bright Cynthia's pow'r divinely great,   95
    What heart is not obeying?
A thousand cupids on her wait
    And in her eyes are playing.

Feminine
ideal

II

She seems the Queen of Love to reign,
    For she alone dispenses   100
Such sweets as best can entertain
    The gust of all the senses.

III

Her face a charming prospect brings,
    Her breath gives balmy blisses;
I hear an angel when she sings   105
    And taste of Heaven in kisses.

IV

Four senses thus she feasts with joy,
    From nature's richest treasure;
Let me the other sense employ
    And I shall die with pleasure.   110

94.2 Leveridge] *Q2–3, H, C1–2,*   107. joy] *all edns.;* joys *DM.*
S; Loverdige *Q1.*
106. Heaven] *all edns.;* Heaven
alone *DM.*

94.1. *Mr. Cheek*] probably Thomas Cheek, Esq., who wrote the text
of "Corinna, I excuse thy face" in V.iii of Southerne's *The Wives
Excuse* (1692).

94.2. *Mr. Leveridge*] Richard Leveridge (ca. 1670–1758) appears to
have sung in both Rich's and Betterton's companies. He had a very
powerful deep bass voice and was later a popular song writer and
composer.

109. *other sense*] i.e., touch.

During the entertainment the Governor, Blanford, Stanmore,
Oroonoko *enter as spectators; that ended,* Captain Driver, Jack
Stanmore, *and several* Planters *enter with their swords drawn.*
A bell rings.

CAPTAIN.

    Where are you, Governor? Make what haste you can
    To save yourself and the whole colony.
    I bid 'em ring the bell.

GOVERNOR.   What's the matter?

JACK STANMORE.

    The Indians are come down upon us.
    They have plundered some of the plantations already   115
    And are marching this way as fast as they can.

GOVERNOR.

    What can we do against 'em?

BLANFORD.

    We shall be able to make a stand
    Till more planters come in to us.

JACK STANMORE.

    There are a great many more without   120
    If you would show yourself and put us in order.

GOVERNOR.

    There's no danger of the white slaves; they'll not stir.
    Blanford and Stanmore, come you along with me.
    Some of you stay here to look after the black slaves.

All go out but the Captain *and six* Planters *who all at once*
seize Oroonoko.

1 PLANTER.

    Ay, ay, let us alone.   125

CAPTAIN.

    In the first place we secure you, sir,
    As an enemy to the government.

OROONOKO (*calling to* Blanford).

    Are you there, sir; you are my constant friend.

1 PLANTER.

    You will be able to do a great deal of mischief.

CAPTAIN.

    But we shall prevent you. Bring the irons hither. He has 130
    the malice of a slave in him and would be glad to be cut-

ting his masters' throats; I know him. Chain his hands
and feet that he may not run over to 'em. If they have
him, they shall carry him on their backs, that I can tell 'em.

As they are chaining him, Blanford *enters, runs to 'em.*

BLANFORD.

What are you doing there?   135
CAPTAIN.

Securing the main chance; this is a bosom enemy.
BLANFORD.

Away, you brutes. I'll answer with my life for his behavior; so tell the Governor.
CAPTAIN AND PLANTERS [*in unison*].

Well, sir, so we will.   *Exeunt* Captain *and* Planters.
OROONOKO.

Give me a sword and I'll deserve your trust.   140

A party of Indians enter hurrying Imoinda *among the slaves;
another party of Indians sustains 'em retreating, followed at a
distance by the* Governor *with the* Planters; Blanford, Oroonoko
join 'em.

BLANFORD.

Hell and the devil! They drive away our slaves before
our faces. Governor, can you stand tamely by and suffer
this? Clemene, sir, your mistress is among 'em.
GOVERNOR.

We throw ourselves away in the attempt to rescue 'em.
OROONOKO.

A lover cannot fall more glorious   145
Than in the cause of love. He that deserves
His mistress's favor wonnot stay behind.
I'll lead you on; be bold and follow me.

147. mistress's] *Q1–3, H;* mistress' *C1;* mistress, *C2, S.*

147. *wonnot*] will not (obsolete).

Oroonoko *at the head of the* Planters *falls upon the* Indians
with a great shout, beats 'em off. Imoinda *enters.*

IMOINDA.

    I'm tossed about by my tempestuous fate
    And nowhere must have rest: Indians or English!   150
    Whoever has me, I am still a slave.
    No matter whose I am, since I am no more
    My royal master's, since I'm his no more.
    O, I was happy! Nay, I will be happy
    In the dear thought that I am still his wife,   155
    Though far divided from him.
                  Draws off to a corner of the stage.

After a shout, enter the Governor *with* Oroonoko, Blanford,
Stanmore, *and the* Planters.

GOVERNOR.

    Thou glorious man! Thou something greater sure
    Than Caesar ever was! That single arm
    Has saved us all; accept our general thanks.
                  All bow to Oroonoko.
    And what we can do more to recompense   160
    Such noble services you shall command.
    Clemene too shall thank you—she is safe—
    Look up and bless your brave deliverer.
        Brings Clemene *forward, looking down on the ground.*

OROONOKO.

    Bless me indeed!

BLANFORD.   You start!

OROONOKO.   O all you gods!

    Who govern this great world and bring about   165
    Things strange and unexpected, can it be?

GOVERNOR.

    What is't you stare at so?

OROONOKO *(looking still fixed on her).*

    Answer me some of you, you who have power
    And have your senses free. Or are you all
    Struck through with wonder too?

BLANFORD.   What would you know? 170

OROONOKO.

    My soul steals from my body through my eyes.
    All that is left of life I'll gaze away
    And die upon the pleasure.

GOVERNOR.   This is strange!

OROONOKO.

    If you but mock me with her image here;
    If she be not Imoinda—

She looks upon him and falls into a swoon; he runs to her.

                Ha! She faints!   175
    Nay, then it must be she. It is Imoinda.
    My heart confesses her and leaps for joy
    To welcome her to her own empire here.
    I feel her all, in every part of me.
    O! Let me press her in my eager arms,   180
    Wake her to life, and with this kindling kiss
    Give back that soul she only sent to me.   *Kisses her.*

GOVERNOR.

    I am amazed!

BLANFORD.   I am as much as you.

OROONOKO.

    Imoinda! O! Thy Oroonoko calls.

                 Imoinda *coming to life.*

IMOINDA.

    My Oroonoko! O! I can't believe   185
    What any man can say. But if I am
    To be deceived, there's something in that name,
    That voice, that face—   *Staring on him.*
              O! If I know myself,
    I cannot be mistaken.   *Runs and embraces* Oroonoko.

OROONOKO.   Never here;

    You cannot be mistaken. I am yours,   190
    Your Oroonoko, all that you would have,
    Your tender loving husband.

IMOINDA.   All indeed

    That I would have: my husband! Then I am
    Alive and waking to the joys I feel;
    They were so great I could not think 'em true.   195
    But I believe all that you say to me.

    For truth itself and everlasting love
    Grows in this breast, and pleasure in these arms.
OROONOKO.
    Take, take me all. Enquire into my heart
    (You know the way to every secret there),   200
    My heart, the sacred treasury of love.
    And if in absence I have misemployed
    A mite from the rich store, if I have spent
    A wish, a sigh, but what I sent to you,
    May I be cursed to wish and sigh in vain,   205
    And you not pity me.
IMOINDA.   O! I believe
    And know you by myself. If these sad eyes
    Since last we parted have beheld the face
    Of any comfort, or once wished to see
    The light of any other heaven but you,   210
    May I be struck this moment blind and lose
    Your blessed sight, never to find you more.
OROONOKO.
    Imoinda! O! This separation
    Has made you dearer, if it can be so,
    Than you were ever to me. You appear   215
    Like a kind star to my benighted steps
    To guide me on my way to happiness:
    I cannot miss it now. Governor, friend,
    You think me mad; but let me bless you all
    Who any way have been the instruments   220
    Of finding her again. Imoinda's found!
    And everything that I would have in her.

        Embracing her in the most passionate fondness.

STANMORE.
    Where's your mistress now, Governor?
GOVERNOR.
    Why, where most men's mistresses are forced to be sometimes,
    with her husband it seems. (*Aside.*) But I won't lose her so. 225
STANMORE.
    He has fought lustily for her and deserves her, I'll say
    that for him.

BLANFORD.

Sir, we congratulate your happiness. I do most heartily.

GOVERNOR.

And all of us. But how it comes to pass—

OROONOKO.

That will require more precious time than I can spare
   you now.   230
I have a thousand things to ask of her,
And she as many more to know of me.
But you have made me happier, I confess,
Acknowledge it, much happier than I
Have words or pow'r to tell you. Captain, you,   235
Ev'n you who most have wronged me, I forgive.
I won't say you have betrayed me now.
I'll think you but the minister of fate
To bring me to my loved Imoinda here.

IMOINDA.

How, how shall I receive you? How be worthy   240
Of such endearments, all this tenderness?
These are the transports of prosperity,
When fortune smiles upon us.

OROONOKO.

Let the fools, who follow fortune, live upon her smiles.
All our prosperity is placed in love.   245
We have enough of that to make us happy.
This little spot of earth you stand upon
Is more to me than the extended plains
Of my great father's kingdom. Here I reign
In full delights, in joys to pow'r unknown;   250
Your love my empire and your heart my throne.   *Exeunt.*

244. fools,] *Q1–3, H, C1, S;* fools
C2.

245–251. *All . . . throne.*] This is a possible echo of Antony's
speech: "Let Rome in Tiber melt, and the wide arch/ Of the rang'd
empire fall! Here is my space./ Kingdoms are clay; our dungy earth
alike/ Feeds beast as man; the nobleness of life/ Is to do thus, when
such a mutual pair . . ." (Shakespeare, *Antony and Cleopatra,* I.i.
33–37).

ACT III

[III.i]

[A Plantation. Enter] Aboan *with several* Slaves, Hottman.

HOTTMAN.

    What! To be slaves to cowards! Slaves to rogues!
    Who can't defend themselves!

ABOAN *(aside to his own gang).*

    Who is this fellow? He talks as if he were acquainted
    With our design. Is he one of us?

SLAVE.

    Not yet, but he will be glad to make one, I believe.   5

ABOAN.

    He makes a mighty noise.

HOTTMAN.

    Go, sneak in corners, whisper out your griefs
    For fear your masters hear you, cringe and crouch
    Under the bloody whip like beaten curs
    That lick their wounds and know no other cure.   10
    All, wretches all! You feel their cruelty
    As much as I can feel, but dare not groan.
    For my part, while I have a life and tongue,
    I'll curse the authors of my slavery.

ABOAN.

    Have you been long a slave?

HOTTMAN.   Yes, many years.   15

ABOAN.

    And do you only curse?

HOTTMAN.

    Curse? Only curse? I cannot conjure
    To raise the spirits of other men.
    I am but one. O! For a soul of fire

---

19. *O . . . fire*] This is an echo of the opening line of the prologue
to Shakespeare's *Henry V:* "O for a Muse of Fire." Hottman's name
may be taken from that of Hotspur in Part 1 of *Henry IV.* He has
no equivalent in Behn's *Oroonoko.*

To warm and animate our common cause   20
And make a body of us. Then I would
Do something more than curse.

ABOAN.

That body set on foot, you would be one,
A limb, to lend it motion?

HOTTMAN.   I would be
The heart of it: the head, the hand, and heart.   25
Would I could see the day!

ABOAN.   You will do all yourself.

HOTTMAN.

I would do more than I shall speak, but I may find a time.

ABOAN.

The time may come to you; be ready for't.
[*Aside.*] Methinks he talks too much. I'll know him more
Before I trust him farther.   30

SLAVE.

If he dares half what he says, he'll be of use to us.

Enter Blanford *to 'em.*

BLANFORD.

If there be anyone among you here
That did belong to Oroonoko, speak;
I come to him.

ABOAN.

I did belong to him. Aboan, my name.   35

BLANFORD.

You are the man I want; pray, come with me.   *Exeunt.*

[III.ii]   [*A room. Enter*] Oroonoko *and* Imoinda.

OROONOKO.

I do not blame my father for his love
(Though that had been enough to ruin me);
'Twas nature's fault that made you like the sun
The reasonable worship of mankind.
He could not help his adoration.   5
Age had not locked his senses up so close
But he had eyes that opened to his soul
And took your beauties in; he felt your pow'r,

And therefore I forgive his loving you.
But when I think on his barbarity   10
That could expose you to so many wrongs,
Driving you out to wretched slavery
Only for being mine, then I confess
I wish I could forget the name of son
That I might curse the tyrant.
IMOINDA.   I will bless him,   15
For I have found you here. Heav'n only knows
What is reserved for us; but if we guess
The future by the past, our fortune must
Be wonderful, above the common size
Of good or ill; it must be in extremes: 20
Extremely happy, or extremely wretched.
OROONOKO.
'Tis in our pow'r to make it happy now.
IMOINDA.
But not to keep it so.

                Enter Blanford *and* Aboan.

BLANFORD.   My royal lord!
I have a present for you.
OROONOKO.   Aboan!
ABOAN.
Your lowest slave.
OROONOKO.   My tried and valued friend.   25
This worthy man always prevents my wants;
I only wished, and he has brought thee to me.
Thou art surprised. Carry thy duty there,

                Aboan *goes to* Imoinda *and falls at her feet.*

While I acknowledge mine; how shall I thank you?
BLANFORD.
Believe me honest to your interest,   30
And I am more than paid. I have secured
That all your followers shall be gently used.
This gentleman, your chiefest favorite,

29. you?] *Q2–3, H,   C1–2, S;*
you. *Q1.*

Shall wait upon your person while you stay
Among us.

OROONOKO. I owe everything to you. 35

BLANFORD.
You must not think you are in slavery.

OROONOKO.
I do not find I am.

BLANFORD.
Kind Heaven has miraculously sent
Those comforts that may teach you to expect
Its farther care in your deliverance. 40

OROONOKO.
I sometimes think myself Heav'n is concerned
For my deliverance.

BLANFORD. It will be soon.
You may expect it. Pray, in the meantime,
Appear as cheerful as you can among us.
You have some enemies that represent 45
You dangerous and would be glad to find
A reason in your discontent to fear.
They watch your looks. But there are honest men
Who are your friends; you are secure in them.

Foreshadowing?

OROONOKO.
I thank you for your caution.

BLANFORD. I will leave you, 50
And be assured I wish your liberty. *Exit.*

ABOAN.
He speaks you very fair.

OROONOKO. He means me fair.

ABOAN.
If he should not, my lord?

OROONOKO. If he should not!
I'll not suspect his truth, but if I did,
What shall I get by doubting?

ABOAN. You secure 55
Not to be disappointed; but besides

There's this advantage in suspecting him:
When you put off the hopes of other men,
You will rely upon your god-like self
And then you may be sure of liberty.   60

OROONOKO.

Be sure of liberty! What dost thou mean
Advising to rely upon myself?
I think I may be sure on't.   *Turning to* Imoinda.
                              We must wait;
'Tis worth a little patience.

ABOAN.   O my lord!

OROONOKO.

What dost thou drive at?

ABOAN.   Sir, another time   65
You would have found it sooner, but I see
Love has your heart and takes up all your thoughts.

OROONOKO.

And canst thou blame me?

ABOAN.   Sir, I must not blame you.
But as our fortune stands there is a passion
[*To* Imoinda.] (Your pardon, royal mistress, I must speak)   70
That would become you better than your love:
A brave resentment, which inspired by you,
Might kindle and diffuse a generous rage
Among the slaves to rouse and shake our chains
And struggle to be free.

OROONOKO.   How can we help ourselves?   75

ABOAN.

I knew you when you would have found a way.
How help ourselves! The very Indians teach us.
We need but to attempt our liberty
And we may carry it. We have hands sufficient,
Double the number of our masters' force,   80
Ready to be employed. What hinders us
To set 'em then at work? We want but you
To head our enterprise and bid us strike.

OROONOKO.

What would you do?

ABOAN.   Cut our oppressors' throats.

OROONOKO.

    And you would have me join in your design   85
    Of murder?

ABOAN.   It deserves a better name.

    But be it what it will, 'tis justified
    By self-defense and natural liberty.

OROONOKO.

    I'll hear no more on't.

ABOAN.   I am sorry for't.

OROONOKO.

    Nor shall you think of it!

ABOAN.   Not think of it!   90

OROONOKO.

    No, I command you not.

ABOAN.   Remember, sir,
    You are a slave yourself, and to command
    Is now another's right. Not think of it!
    Since the first moment they put on my chains,
    I've thought of nothing but the weight of 'em   95
    And how to throw 'em off. Can yours fit easy?

OROONOKO.

    I have a sense of my condition
    As painful and as quick as yours can be.
    I feel for my Imoinda and myself,
    Imoinda much the tenderest part of me.   100
    But though I languish for my liberty,
    I would not buy it at the Christian price
    Of black ingratitude. They shannot say

90. it!] it. *all edns.*

---

88. *self-defense and natural liberty*] According to Thomas Hobbes,
a slave might do anything to gain his freedom since he was in a condition of perpetual war with his master (*Leviathan,* ed. A. R. Waller
[Cambridge, 1935], p. 142). Aboan's arguments and language are
reminiscent of Pierre's in Otway's *Venice Preserved* (1682): "Nay, it's
a cause thou wilt be fond of, Jaffeir./ For it is founded on the
noblest basis,/ Our liberties, our natural inheritance" (ed. Malcolm
Kelsall [Lincoln, Nebr., 1969], II.ii.88–89).

103. *black ingratitude*] Thomas Tryon has his slaves argue that
revolt was natural enough for slaves, but this did not mean that they
might be permitted to do anything which went against their inner

That we deserved our fortune by our crimes.
Murder the innocent!

ABOAN.   The innocent!   105

OROONOKO.

These men are so whom you would rise against.
If we are slaves, they did not make us slaves,
But bought us in an honest way of trade
As we have done before 'em, bought and sold
Many a wretch and never thought it wrong.   110
They paid our price for us and we are now
Their property, a part of their estate,
To manage as they please. Mistake me not;
I do not tamely say that we should bear
All they could lay upon us, but we find   115
The load so light, so little to be felt
(Considering they have us in their pow'r
And may inflict what grievances they please),
We ought not to complain.

ABOAN.   My royal lord!

You do not know the heavy grievances,   120
The toils, the labors, weary drudgeries
Which they impose; burdens more fit for beasts,
For senseless beasts to bear than thinking men.
Then if you saw the bloody cruelties
They execute on every slight offense,   125
Nay, sometimes in their proud, insulting sport,
How worse than dogs they lash their fellow creatures,
Your heart would bleed for 'em. O could you know
How many wretches lift their hands and eyes
To you for their relief!

OROONOKO.   I pity 'em   130
And wish I could with honesty do more.

---

sense of morality, or what Tryon has them call their "selves" (*The Negro's Complaint of Their Hard Servitude* [London, 1684], pp. 111–14, 118–19).

103. *shannot*] shall not (obsolete).

109. *As we have done*] Behn's Oroonoko had been responsible for selling most of the Africans in Surinam into bondage (Behn, 5: 170).

112. *Their property*] In Behn's novella, Oroonoko tries to buy his freedom with "either Gold, or a vast Quantity of Slaves" (Behn, 5: 175).

ABOAN.

You must do more, and may with honesty.
O royal sir, remember who you are,
A prince, born for the good of other men,
Whose god-like office is to draw the sword   135
Against oppression and set free mankind,
And this I'm sure you think oppression now.
What though you have not felt these miseries,
Never believe you are obliged to them.
They have their selfish reasons, maybe, now   140
For using of you well, but there will come
A time when you must have your share of 'em.

OROONOKO.

You see how little cause I have to think so:
Favored in my own person, in my friends,
Indulged in all that can concern my care,   145
In my Imoinda's soft society.   *Embracing her.*

ABOAN.

And therefore would you lie contented down
In the forgetfulness and arms of love
To get young princes for 'em?

OROONOKO.   Say'st thou! Ha!

ABOAN.

Princes, the heirs of empire and the last   150
Of your illustrious lineage, to be born
To pamper up their pride and be their slaves!

OROONOKO.

Imoinda! Save me, save me from that thought.

IMOINDA.

There is no safety from it. I have long
Suffered it with a mother's laboring pains   155
And can no longer. Kill me, kill me now
While I am blest and happy in your love
Rather than let me live to see you hate me,
As you must hate me—me, the only cause,
The fountain of these flowing miseries.   160
Dry up this spring of life, this pois'nous spring
That swells so fast to overwhelm us all.

152. slaves!] slaves? *all edns.*   159. me—] me; *all edns.*

OROONOKO.

> Shall the dear babe, the eldest of my hopes,
> Whom I begot a prince be born a slave?
> The treasure of this temple was designed   165
> T'enrich a kingdom's fortune. Shall it here
> Be seized upon by vile unhallowed hands
> To be employed in uses most profane?

ABOAN.

> In most unworthy uses. Think of that,
> And while you may, prevent it. O my lord!   170
> Rely on nothing that they say to you.
> They speak you fair, I know, and bid you wait.
> But think what 'tis to wait on promises,
> And promises of men who know no tie
> Upon their words against their interest.   175
> And where's their interest in freeing you?

IMOINDA.

> O! Where indeed, to lose so many slaves?

ABOAN.

> Nay, grant this man you think so much your friend
> Be honest and intends all that he says;
> He is but one, and in a government   180
> Where he confesses you have enemies
> That watch your looks. What looks can you put on
> To please these men who are before resolved
> To read 'em their own way? Alas! My lord!
> If they incline to think you dangerous,   185
> They have their knavish arts to make you so.
> And then who knows how far their cruelty
> May carry their revenge?

IMOINDA.   To everything

> That does belong to you, your friends, and me;
> I shall be torn from you, forced away,   190

178. Nay.] *Q3, H, C1–2, S;* Nay   184. own] *H;* own own *Q1–3,*
Q1–2.   *C1–2, S.*

---

177. *so many slaves*] Behn tells us that the pregnant Imoinda
"believ'd, if it were so hard to gain the Liberty of two, 'twould be
more difficult to get that for three" (Behn, 5: 189).

Helpless and miserable. Shall I live
To see that day again?

OROONOKO.   That day shall never come.

ABOAN.

    I know you are persuaded to believe
    The governor's arrival will prevent
    These mischiefs and bestow your liberty.   195
    But who is sure of that? I rather fear
    More mischiefs from his coming. He is young,
    Luxurious, passionate, and amorous;
    Such a complexion and made bold by pow'r
    To countenance all he is prone to do   200
    Will know no bounds, no law against his lusts.
    If in a fit of his intemperance,
    With a strong hand he should resolve to seize
    And force my royal mistress from your arms,
    How can you help yourself?

OROONOKO.   Ha! Thou hast roused   205
    The lion in his den; he stalks abroad
    And the wide forest trembles at his roar.
    I find the danger now; my spirits start
    At the alarm and from all quarters come
    To man my heart, the citadel of love.   210
    Is there a pow'r on earth to force you from me?
    And shall I not resist it? Not strike first
    To keep, to save you? To prevent that curse?
    This is your cause, and shall it not prevail?
    O! You were born all ways to conquer me.   215
    Now I am fashioned to thy purpose. Speak,
    What combination, what conspiracy,
    Wouldst thou engage me in? I'll undertake
    All thou wouldst have me now for liberty,
    For the great cause of love and liberty.   220

ABOAN.

    Now, my great master, you appear yourself.
    And since we have you joined in our design,
    It cannot fail us. I have mustered up

he's convinced

213. you?] *Q1–2;* you; *Q3, H,*
C1–2, S.

    The choicest slaves, men who are sensible

    Of their condition and seem most resolved.   225

    They have their several parties.

OROONOKO.   Summon 'em,

    Assemble 'em; I will come forth and show

    Myself among 'em. If they are resolved,

    I'll lead their foremost resolutions.

ABOAN.

    I have provided those will follow you.   230

OROONOKO.

    With this reserve in our proceeding still,

    The means that lead us to our liberty

    Must not be bloody.

ABOAN.   You command in all.

    We shall expect you, sir.

OROONOKO.   You shannot long.

Exeunt Oroonoko *and* Imoinda *at one door,* Aboan *at another.*

[III.iii]   Welldon *coming in before* Mrs. Lackitt.

WIDOW.

    These unmannerly Indians were something unseasonable

    to disturb us just in the nick, Mr. Welldon, but I have

    the parson within call still to do us the good turn.

WELLDON.

    We had best stay a little, I think, to see things settled

    again, had not we? Marriage is a serious thing, you   5

    know.

WIDOW.

    What do you talk of a serious thing, Mr. Welldon? I

    think you have found me sufficiently serious. I have

    married my son to your sister to pleasure you; and now

    I come to claim your promise to me, you tell me marriage   10

    is a serious thing.

WELLDON.

    Why, is it not?

    231–33. *With . . . bloody.*] This is a possible echo of Brutus' vain
wish in Shakespeare's *Julius Caesar*: "Let us be sacrificers, but not
butchers, Caius./ We all stand up against the spirit of Caesar,/ And
in the spirit of men there is no blood" (II.i.166–68).

WIDOW.

Fiddle faddle, I know what it is. 'Tis not the first time
I have been married, I hope; but I shall begin to think
you don't design to do fairly by me, so I shall.   15

WELLDON.

Why indeed, Mrs. Lackitt, I am afraid I can't do as fairly
as I would by you. 'Tis what you must know, first or
last, and I should be the worst man in the world to con-
ceal it any longer; therefore I must own to you that I
am married already.   20

WIDOW.

Married! You don't say so I hope! How have you the
conscience to tell me such a thing to my face! Have you
abused me then, fooled and cheated me? What do you
take me for, Mr. Welldon? Do you think I am to be
served at this rate? But you shan't find me the silly   25
creature you think me. I would have you to know I
understand better things than to ruin my son without
a valuable consideration. If I can't have you, I can keep
my money. Your sister shan't have the catch of him she
expected. I won't part with a shilling to 'em.   30

WELLDON.

You made the match yourself, you know; you can't
blame me.

WIDOW.

Yes, yes, I can and do blame you; you might have told
me before you were married.

WELLDON.

I would not have told you now, but you followed me so   35
close I was forced to't. Indeed I am married in England, but 'tis as if I were not, for I have been parted
from my wife a great while. And to do reason on both
sides, we hate one another heartily. Now I did design
and will marry you still, if you'll have a little patience. 40

WIDOW.

A likely business truly. ⟶ 101

WELLDON.

I have a friend in England that I will write to, to poison
my wife, and then I can marry you with a good con-

WHAT

science. If you love me, as you say you do, you'll consent
to that, I'm sure.   45

WIDOW.

And will he do it, do you think?

WELLDON.

At the first word, or he is not the man I take him to be.

WIDOW.

Well, you are a dear devil, Mr. Welldon, and would you
poison your wife for me?

WELLDON.

I would do anything for you.   50

WIDOW.

Well, I am mightily obliged to you. But 'twill be a great
while before you can have an answer of your letter.

WELLDON.

'Twill be a great while indeed.

WIDOW.

In the meantime, Mr. Welldon—

WELLDON.

Why in the meantime—here's company; we'll settle that   55
within. I'll follow you.   *Exit* Widow.

Enter Stanmore.

STANMORE.

So, sir, you carry your business swimmingly. You have
stolen a wedding, I hear.

WELLDON.

Ay, my sister is married, and I am very near being run
away with myself.   60

STANMORE.

The widow will have you then.

WELLDON.

You come very seasonably to my rescue. Jack Stanmore
is to be had, I hope.

STANMORE.

At half an hour's warning.

55. meantime]   *Q1–3*,   *C1–2*,   *S;*
men time *H*.

WELLDON.

    I must advise with you.   *Exeunt.* 65

[III.iv]
[*A Plantation. Enter*] Oroonoko *with* Aboan, Hottman, Slaves.

OROONOKO.

    Impossible! Nothing's impossible.
    We know our strength only by being tried.
    If you object the mountains, rivers, woods
    Unpassable that lie before our march:
    Woods we can set on fire, we swim by nature.   5
    What can oppose us then, but we may tame?
    All things submit to virtuous industry;
    That we can carry with us, that is ours.

SLAVE.

    Great sir, we have attended all you said
    With silent joy and admiration   10
    And, were we only men, would follow such,
    So great a leader, through the untried world.
    But, O! Consider we have other names,
    Husbands and fathers, and have things more dear
    To us than life, our children and our wives,   15
    Unfit for such an expedition.
    What must become of them?

OROONOKO.   We wonnot wrong
    The virtue of our women to believe
    There is a wife among 'em would refuse
    To share her husband's fortune. What is hard   20
    We must make easy to 'em in our love. While we live
    And have our limbs, we can take care for them;
    Therefore I still propose to lead our march
    Down to the sea and plant a colony
    Where, in our native innocence, we shall live   25
    Free and be able to defend ourselves

22. for] *Q1–3, H, S;* of *C1–2.*

---

9. S.P. *Slave*] In Behn's *Oroonoko* the slave who takes this role is
named Tuscan.

Till stress of weather or some accident
Provide a ship for us.
ABOAN.   An accident!
The luckiest accident presents itself.
The very ship that brought and made us slaves   30
Swims in the river still; I see no cause
But we may seize on that.
OROONOKO.   It shall be so.
There is a justice in it pleases me.
(*To the* Slaves.) Do you agree to it?
OMNES.   We follow you.
OROONOKO (*to* Hottman).
You do not relish it.
HOTTMAN.   I am afraid   35
You'll find it difficult and dangerous.
ABOAN.
Are you the man to find the danger first?
You should have giv'n example. Dangerous!
I thought you had not understood the word,
You, who would be the head, the hand, and heart.   40
Sir, I remember you, you can talk well;
I wonnot doubt but you'll maintain your word.
OROONOKO (*aside to* Aboan).
This fellow is not right, I'll try him further.—
[*Aloud.*] The danger will be certain to us all,
And death most certain in miscarrying.   45
We must expect no mercy if we fail;
Therefore our way must be not to expect.
We'll put it out of expectation
By death upon the place or liberty.
There is no mean, but death or liberty.   50
There's no man here, I hope, but comes prepared
For all that can befall him.
                            [Oroonoko *stares at* Hottman.]
ABOAN.   Death is all:
In most conditions of humanity
To be desired, but to be shunned in none;

52. S.P. ABOAN] *Q3, H, C1–2,
S; Oro[onoko] Q1–2.*

The remedy of many, wish of some,   55
And certain end of all.
If there be one among us who can fear
The face of death appearing like a friend,
As in this cause of honor death must be,
How will he tremble when he sees him dressed   60
In the wild fury of our enemies,
In all the terrors of their cruelty?
For now if we should fall into their hands,
Could they invent a thousand murd'ring ways
By racking torments, we should feel 'em all.   65

HOTTMAN.
    What will become of us?
OROONOKO (*aside to* Aboan). Observe him now.
    [*Aloud.*] I could die altogether, like a man,
    As you, and you, and all of us may do;
    But who can promise for his bravery
    Upon the rack, where fainting, weary life,   70
    Hunted through every limb, is forced to feel
    An agonizing death of all its parts?
    Who can bear this? Resolve to be impaled?
    His skin flayed off and roasted yet alive?
    The quivering flesh torn from his broken bones   75
    By burning pincers? Who can bear these pains?

HOTTMAN (*discovering all the confusion of fear*).
    They are not to be borne.

OROONOKO.
    You see him now, this man of mighty words!

ABOAN.
    How his eyes roll!

OROONOKO.   He cannot hide his fear.
    I tried him this way and have found him out.   80

ABOAN.
    I could not have believed it. Such a blaze,
    And not a spark of fire!

OROONOKO.   His violence
    Made me suspect him first; now I'm convinced.

70. rack,] rack? *all edns.*   77. borne] born *all edns.*

ABOAN.

    What shall we do with him?

OROONOKO.   He is not fit—

ABOAN.

    Fit! Hang him, he is only fit to be   85
    Just what he is, to live and die a slave,
    The base companion of his servile fears.

OROONOKO.

    We are not safe with him.

ABOAN.   Do you think so?

OROONOKO.

    He'll certainly betray us.

ABOAN.   That he shan't.
    I can take care of that; I have a way   90
    To take him off his evidence.

OROONOKO.   What way?

ABOAN.

    I'll stop his mouth before you, stab him here,
    And then let him inform.

                Going to stab Hottman, Oroonoko *holds him.*

OROONOKO.   Thou art not mad?

ABOAN.

    I would secure ourselves.

OROONOKO.

    It shannot be this way, nay cannot be.   95
    His murder would alarm all the rest,
    Make 'em suspect us of barbarity,
    And, maybe, fall away from our design.
    We'll not set out in blood.
        [*Addressing the* Slaves.] We have, my friends,
    This night to furnish what we can provide   100
    For our security and just defense.
    If there be one among us we suspect
    Of baseness or vile fear, it will become
    Our common care to have our eyes on him.
    I wonnot name the man.

ABOAN (*to* Hottman).   You guess at him.   105

OROONOKO.

    Tomorrow, early as the breaking day,

We rendezvous behind the citron grove.
That ship secured, we may transport ourselves
To our respective homes. My father's kingdom
Shall open her wide arms to take you in   110
And nurse you for her own, adopt you all,
All who will follow me.

OMNES.   All, all follow you.

OROONOKO.

There I can give you all your liberty,
Bestow its blessings, and secure 'em yours.
There you shall live with honor, as becomes   115
My fellow sufferers and worthy friends.
This if we do succeed. But if we fall
In our attempt, 'tis nobler still to die
Then drag the galling yoke of slavery.   *Exeunt omnes.*

ACT IV

[IV.i]   [*Enter*] Welldon *and* Jack Stanmore.

WELLDON.

You see, honest Jack, I have been industrious for you;
you must take some pains now to serve yourself.

JACK STANMORE.

Gad, Mr. Welldon, I have taken a great deal of pains;
and if the widow speaks honestly, faith and troth, she'll
tell you what a pains-taker I am.   5

WELLDON.

Fie, fie, not me. I am her husband you know; she won't
tell me what pains you have taken with her. Besides,
she takes you for me.

JACK STANMORE.

That's true; I forgot you had married her. But if you
knew all—   10

WELLDON.

'Tis no matter for my knowing all, if she does—

JACK STANMORE.

Ay, ay, she does know, and more than ever she knew
since she was a woman, for the time; I will be bold to
say, for I have done—

WELLDON.

The devil take you, for you'll never have done.   15

JACK STANMORE.

As old as she is, she has a wrinkle behind more than

15. you, for] *Q3, H, C1–2;* you,
Q1–2, S.

---

16. *wrinkle*] a trick or wile, here meant in a sexual sense. In Swift's
A Compleat Collection of Genteel and Ingenious Conversation, in *Prose
Works,* ed. Herbert Davis and Louis Landa (Oxford, 1957), [IV], p. 156,
Mr. Neverout gets Miss Notable to confess that she had not heard one
of his proverbs. He then replies, "Why then, Miss, you have one

she had, I believe—for I have taught her what she never
knew in her life before.

WELLDON.

What care I what wrinkles she has? Or what you have
taught her? If you'll let me advise you, you may; if 20
not, you may prate on and ruin the whole design.

JACK STANMORE.

Well, well, I have done.

WELLDON.

Nobody but your cousin and you and I know anything
of this matter. I have married Mrs. Lackitt and put you
to bed to her, which she knows nothing of, to serve you. 25
In two or three days I'll bring it about so to resign up
my claim, with her consent, quietly to you.

JACK STANMORE.

But how will you do it?

WELLDON.

That must be my business. In the meantime, if you
should make any noise, 'twill come to her ears and be 30
impossible to reconcile her.

JACK STANMORE.

Nay, as for that, I know the way to reconcile her, I
warrant you.

WELLDON.

But how will you get her money? I am married to her.

JACK STANMORE.

That I don't know indeed. 35

WELLDON.

You must leave it to me; you find all the pains I shall
put you to will be to be silent. You can hold your tongue
for two or three days?

JACK STANMORE.

Truly not well in a matter of this nature. I should be
very unwilling to lose the reputation of this night's work 40
and the pleasure of telling.

---

wrinkle—more than ever you had before." Swift's version may itself
have sexual connotations playing with wrinkle as a fold, particularly a
fold in the skin, and a trick; but the sexual reference of *behind* and
before (ll. 16–18) in Southerne's play seems obvious.

WELLDON.

You must mortify that vanity a little. You will have time
enough to brag and lie of your manhood when you have
her in a bare-faced condition to disprove you.

JACK STANMORE.

Well, I'll try what I can do. The hopes of her money   45
must do it.

WELLDON.

You'll come at night again? 'Tis your own business.

JACK STANMORE.

But you have the credit on't.

WELLDON.

'Twill be your own another day, as the widow says. Send
your cousin to me; I want his advice.   50

JACK STANMORE.

I want to be recruited, I'm sure, a good breakfast and
to bed. She has rocked my cradle sufficiently.   *Exit.*

WELLDON.

She would have a husband, and if all be as he says, she
has no reason to complain; but there's no relying on
what the men say upon these occasions. They have the   55
benefit of their bragging by recommending their abilities
to other women. Theirs is a trading estate that lives upon
credit and increases by removing it out of one bank
into another. Now poor women have not these opportunities. We must keep our stocks dead by us at home   60

57–59. *Theirs . . . another.*] The Bank of England was established
in 1694, but as Defoe's section "Of Banks" in *An Essay upon Projects*
reveals, the Bank of England did not solve the need for easy access to
credit. Nevertheless, the use of bills of credit from merchants allowed
them to operate far beyond the immediate cash they had on hand. As
Defoe put it some years later in his *Review*, "Credit has made Paper
pay Millions instead of Money, doubled and trebled our Specie by
Circulation; Credit has brought out our Hoards, melted down our
Plate, sold our Jewels to take Air for Silver, and split Stick for Gold;
Credit has paid Interest for nothing, and turn'd nothing into something, Coin'd Paper into Metal, and stampt a Value upon what had
no Value before." See *An Essay upon Projects*, in *The Earlier Life
and Works of Daniel Defoe*, ed. Henry Morley (London, 1889), pp.
46–58; and *Review*, ed. Arthur Wellesley Secord, Vol. 7, no. 55,
Facsimile Book 17 (New York, 1938), p. 214.

to be ready for a purchase when it comes, a husband,
let him be never so dear, and be glad of him; or venture
our fortunes abroad on such rotten security that the
principal and interest, nay, very often our persons, are
in danger. If the women would agree (which they never   65
will) to call home their effects, how many proper gentlemen would sneak into another way of living for want
of being responsible in this? Then husbands would be
cheaper. Here comes the widow; she'll tell truth. She'll
not bear false witness against her own interest, I know.   70

Enter Widow Lackitt.

WELLDON.

Now, Mrs. Lackitt.

WIDOW.

Well, well, Lackitt, or what you will now—now I am
married to you. I am very well pleased with what I have
done, I assure you.

WELLDON.

And with what I have done too, I hope.   75

WIDOW.

Ah! Mr. Welldon! I say nothing, but you're a dear man,
and I did not think it had been in you.

WELLDON.

I have more in me than you imagine.

WIDOW.

No, no, you can't have more than I imagine. 'Tis impossible to have more. You have enough for any woman   80
in an honest way, that I will say for you.

WELLDON.

Then I find you are satisfied.

---

63. *rotten*] unsound.
66. *their effects*] Behind the imagery of trade is a complaint
against the double standard by which men achieve a reputation by
having many affairs, while women, if they are driven to having affairs
by lack of a husband, run the risk of ruined reputations as well as
venereal disease. The call for united abstention from sex in the
manner of Aristophanes' *Lysistrata* has, as Charlotte admits, little
chance of success.

WIDOW.

Satisfied! No indeed; I'm not to be satisfied with you or
without you. To be satisfied is to have enough of you.
Now, 'tis a folly to lie; I shall never think I can have   85
enough of you. I shall be very fond of you. Would you
have me fond of you? What do you do to me to make
me love you so well?

WELLDON.

Can't you tell what?

WIDOW.

Go, there's no speaking to you. You bring all the blood   90
of one's body into one's face, so you do. Why do you
talk so?

WELLDON.

Why, how do I talk?

WIDOW.

You know how, but a little color becomes me, I believe.
How do I look today?   95

WELLDON.

O! Most lovingly, most amiably.

WIDOW.

Nay, this can't be long a secret, I find; I shall discover
it by my countenance.

WELLDON.

The women will find you out, you look so cheerfully.

WIDOW.

But do I, do I really look so cheerfully, so amiably?   100
There's no such paint in the world as the natural glow-
ing of a complexion. Let 'em find me out, if they please,
poor creatures, I pity 'em. They envy me, I'm sure, and
would be glad to mend their looks upon the same occasion. The young jill-flirting girls, forsooth, believe no- 105
body must have a husband but themselves, but I would
have 'em to know there are other things to be taken care
of besides their green sickness.

---

87. *fond*] foolishly affectionate.
108. *green sickness*] "an anemic disease which mostly affects young
women about the age of puberty and gives a pale or greenish tinge
to their complexion" (*OED*). As used by Widow Lackitt, it applies to
women who have not yet had any sexual experience.

WELLDON.

Ay, sure, or the physicians would have but little practice.   110

WIDOW.

Mr. Welldon, what must I call you? I must have some
pretty fond name or other for you. What shall I call you?

WELLDON.

I thought you liked my own name.

WIDOW.

Yes, yes, I like it, but I must have a nickname for you.
Most women have nicknames for their husbands—   115

WELLDON.

Cuckold.

WIDOW.

No, no, but 'tis very pretty before company; it looks
negligent and is the fashion, you know.

WELLDON.

To be negligent of their husbands, it is indeed.

WIDOW.

Nay then, I won't be in the fashion, for I can never be   120
negligent of dear Mr. Welldon; and to convince you,
here's something to encourage you not to be negligent
of me.   *Gives him a purse and a little casket.*
Five hundred pounds in gold in this, and jewels to the
value of five hundred pounds more in this.   125
                              Welldon *opens the casket.*

WELLDON.

Ay, marry, this will encourage me indeed.

WIDOW.

There are comforts in marrying an elderly woman, Mr.
Welldon. Now a young woman would have fancied she
had paid you with her person or had done you the favor.

WELLDON.

What do you talk of young women? You are as young 130
as any of 'em in everything but their folly and ignorance.

WIDOW.

And do you think me so? But I have no reason to suspect

132. think] *Q2-3, H, C1-2, S;*
thing *Q1.*

you. Was not I seen at your house this morning, do you think?

WELLDON.

You may venture again; you'll come at night, I suppose. 135

WIDOW.

O dear! At night? So soon?

WELLDON.

Nay, if you think it so soon.

WIDOW.

O! No, it is not for that, Mr. Welldon, but—

WELLDON.

You won't come then.

WIDOW.

Won't! I don't say I won't. That is not a word for a 140
wife. If you command me—

WELLDON.

To please yourself.

WIDOW.

I will come to please you.

WELLDON.

To please yourself, own it.

WIDOW.

Well, well, to please myself then. You're the strangest 145
man in the world, nothing can 'scape you. You'll to
the bottom of everything.

Enter Daniel, Lucy *following.*

DANIEL.

What would you have? What do you follow me for?

LUCY.

Why, mayn't I follow you? I must follow you now all
the world over.   150

DANIEL.

Hold you, hold you there, not so far by a mile or two;
I have enough of your company already, by'r'lady,
and something to spare. You may go home to your
brother, an' you will, I have no farther to do with you.

154. an'] *Q2*; an *Q1, Q3, H,*
C1–2, S.

WIDOW.

> Why, Daniel, child, thou art not out of thy wits sure, 155
> art thou?

DANIEL.

> Nay, marry, I don't know, but I am very near it, I
> believe. I am altered for the worse mightily since you
> saw me, and she has been the cause of it there.

WIDOW.

> How so, child?   160

DANIEL.

> I told you before what would come on't, of putting me
> to bed to a strange woman, but you would not be said
> nay.

WIDOW.

> She is your wife now, child; you must love her.

DANIEL.

> Why, so I did, at first.   165

WIDOW.

> But you must love her always.

DANIEL.

> Always! I loved her as long as I could, mother, and as
> long as loving was good, I believe, for I find now I
> don't care a fig for her.

LUCY.

> Why, you lubberly, slovenly, misbegotten blockhead—   170

WIDOW.

> Nay, Mistress Lucy, say anything else and spare not; but
> as to his begetting, that touches me; he is as honestly
> begotten, though I say it, that he is the worse again.

LUCY.

> I see all good nature is thrown away upon you—

WIDOW.

> It was so with his father before him. He takes after him. 175

157. it] *Q1–2; om. Q3, H, C1–2,*   172. me;] me, *Q1–3, C1–2, S;*
S.   me: *H.*

173. *the worse again*] so much the worse for being the true child
of his foolish father.

LUCY.

And therefore I will use you as you deserve, you tony.

WIDOW.

Indeed he deserves bad enough, but don't call him out of his name. His name is Daniel, you know.

DANIEL.

She may call me hermaphrodite if she will, for I hardly know whether I'm a boy or a girl.   180

WELLDON.

A boy, I warrant thee, as long as thou livest.

DANIEL.

Let her call me what she pleases, mother; 'tis not her tongue that I am afraid of.

LUCY.

I will make such a beast of thee, such a cuckold!

WIDOW.

O, pray, no, I hope; do nothing rashly, Mrs. Lucy.   185

LUCY.

Such a cuckold will I make of thee!

DANIEL.

I had rather be a cuckold than what you would make of me in a week, I'm sure. I have no more manhood left in me already than there is, saving the mark, in one of my mother's old under-petticoats here.   190

WIDOW.

Sirrah, sirrah, meddle with your wife's petticoats and let your mother's alone, you ungracious bird, you.   *Beats him.*

DANIEL.

Why, is the devil in the woman? What have I said now? Do you know, if you were asked, I trow? But you are all of a bundle. Even hang together. He that unties you 195 makes a rod for his own tail, and so he will find it that

186. will I] *Q1–2;* I will *Q3, H,*   193. Why,] *Q2;* Why *Q1, Q3, H,*
C1–2, S.   *C1–2, S.*

___

176. *tony*] simpleton.
192. *bird*] young man.
196. *own tail*] a proverbial expression for one who by his own acts selects the means by which he is punished. Southerne is not the first to apply it to choosing a wife (Tilley, R 153).

has anything to do with you.

WIDOW.

Ay, rogue enough, you shall find it. I have a rod for
your tail still.

DANIEL.

No wife and I care not.   200

WIDOW.

I'll swinge you into better manners, you booby.

Beats him off. Exit.

WELLDON.

You have consummated our project upon him.

LUCY.

Nay, if I have a limb of the fortune, I care not who has
the whole body of the fool.

WELLDON.

That you shall, and a large one, I promise you.   205

LUCY.

Have you heard the news? They talk of an English ship
in the river.

WELLDON.

I have heard on't and am preparing to receive it as fast
as I can.

LUCY.

There's something the matter too with the slaves, some   210
disturbance or other; I don't know what 'tis.

WELLDON.

So much the better still. We fish in troubled waters; we

200. No wife] *C1-2, S;* No, wife
Q1; No wife, *Q2-3, H.*

---

201. *swinge*] beat, thrash.
202. *consummated*] finished, with the overtones of having consummated the marriage. In this sense, there is a distinct implication of
an aggressive sexual role for Lucy.
212-13. *fish . . . us*] a proverbial expression about finding private
benefit in public disturbance (Tilley, F 334). In The Second Part of
Absalom and Achitophel (1682), Dryden speaks of those "Who Rich
and Great by past Rebellions grew,/ And long to fish the troubled
Streams anew" (ed. H. T. Swedenberg, Jr., and Vinton A. Dearing,
The Works of John Dryden, 2 [Berkeley and Los Angeles, 1972]: 71,
ll. 314-15).

shall have fewer eyes upon us. Pray, go you home and
be ready to assist me in your part of the design.

LUCY.

I can't fail in mine. *Exit.* 215

WELLDON.

The widow has furnished me, I thank her, to carry it on.
Now I have got a wife, 'tis high time to think of getting a husband. I carry my fortune about me: a thousand
pounds in gold and jewels. Let me see—. 'Twill be a
considerable trust, and I think I shall lay it out to 220
advantage.

Enter Stanmore.

STANMORE.

So, Welldon, Jack has told me his success and his hopes
of marrying the widow by your means.

WELLDON.

I have strained a point, Stanmore, upon your account
to be serviceable to your family. 225

STANMORE.

I take it upon my account and am very much obliged
to you. But here we are all in an uproar.

WELLDON.

So they say. What's the matter?

STANMORE.

A mutiny among the slaves. Oroonoko is at the head of
'em; our governor is gone out with his rascally militia 230
against 'em. What it may come to nobody knows.

WELLDON.

For my part I shall do as well as the rest, but I'm concerned for my sister and cousin, whom I expect in the
ship from England.

STANMORE.

There's no danger of 'em. 235

WELLDON.

I have a thousand pounds here in gold and jewels for

236. S.P.   WELLDON]   *Q1–2*,   *H*,
C2, *S*;   *Wid[ow]*   *Q3*, *C1*.

---

220. *trust*] "an estate committed to the charge of trustees" (*OED*).

my cousin's use that I would more particularly take care
of. 'Tis too great a sum to venture at home, and I
would not have her wronged of it; therefore, to secure
it I think my best way will be to put it into your 240
keeping.

STANMORE.

You have a very good opinion of my honesty.

Takes the purse and casket.

WELLDON.

I have indeed; if anything should happen to me in this
bustle, as nobody is secure of accidents, I know you will
take my cousin into your protection and care. 245

STANMORE.

You may be sure on't.

WELLDON.

If you hear she is dead, as she may be, then I desire you
to accept of the thousand pound as a legacy and token
of my friendship. My sister is provided for.

STANMORE.

Why, you amaze me, but you are never the nearer dying, 250
I hope, for making your will?

WELLDON.

Not a jot, but I love to be beforehand with fortune.
If she comes safe, this is not a place for a single woman,
you know. Pray see her married as soon as you can.

STANMORE.

If she be as handsome as her picture, I can promise her 255
a husband.

WELLDON.

If you like her when you see her, I wish nothing so
much as to have you marry her yourself.

STANMORE.

From what I have heard of her and my engagements to
you, it must be her fault if I don't. I hope to have her 260
from your own hand.

WELLDON.

And I hope to give her to you, for all this.

247. S.P. WELLDON] *Q1–2, H,*
C2, S; Wid[ow] Q3, C1.

STANMORE.

Ay, ay, hang these melancholy reflections. Your generosity has engaged all my services.

WELLDON.

I always thought you worth making a friend.   265

STANMORE.

You shan't find your good opinion thrown away upon me. I am in your debt and shall think so as long as I live.   *Exeunt.*

[IV.ii]   [*A grove—moonlight.*]

Enter on one side of the stage Oroonoko, Aboan, *with the slaves,* Imoinda *with a bow and quiver, the* Women, *some leading, others carrying their children upon their backs.*

OROONOKO.

The women with their children fall behind.

Imoinda, you must not expose yourself.

Retire, my love. I almost fear for you.

IMOINDA.

I fear no danger. Life or death I will

Enjoy with you.

OROONOKO.   My person is your guard.   5

ABOAN.

Now, sir, blame yourself. If you had not prevented my cutting his throat, that coward there had not discovered us; he comes now to upbraid you.

Enter on the other side Governor, *talking to* Hottman, *with his rabble.*

GOVERNOR *(to* Hottman).

This is the very thing I would have wished.

Your honest service to the government   10

Shall be rewarded with your liberty.

ABOAN.

His honest service! Call it what it is,

0.3–0.4. *Imoinda . . . backs*] These details are mentioned by Behn. Imoinda actually wounds several settlers including the Governor with her poisoned arrows (Behn, 5: 193–95).

His villainy, the service of his fear.
If he pretends to honest services,
Let him stand out and meet me like a man. *Advancing.* 15
OROONOKO.
Hold, you! And you who come against us, hold!
I charge you in a general good to all
And wish I could command you to prevent
The bloody havoc of the murdering sword.
I would not urge destruction uncompelled, 20
But if you follow fate, you find it here.
The bounds are set, the limits of our lives.
Between us lies the gaping gulf of death
To swallow all. Who first advances—

Enter the Captain *with his crew.*

CAPTAIN.
Here, here, here they are, Governor. 25
What! Seize upon my ship!
Come, boys, fall on—

Advancing first, Oroonoko *kills him.*

OROONOKO.
Thou art fall'n indeed. Thy own blood be upon thee.
GOVERNOR.
Rest it there. He did deserve his death.
Take him away. *The body removed.* 30
You see, sir, you and those mistaken men
Must be our witnesses; we do not come
As enemies and thirsting for your blood.
If we desired your ruin, the revenge
Of our companion's death had pushed it on. 35
But that we overlook in a regard
To common safety and the public good.
OROONOKO.
Regard that public good. Draw off your men
And leave us to our fortune. We're resolved.

16. you] you: *Q1, Q3, H, C1–2,* 16. hold!] hold; *all edns.*
S; you; *Q2.*

GOVERNOR.

    Resolved! On what? Your resolutions   40
    Are broken, overturned, prevented, lost.
    What fortune now can you raise out of 'em?
    Nay, grant we should draw off, what can you do?
    Where can you move? What more can you resolve?
    Unless it be to throw yourselves away.   45
    Famine must eat you up if you go on.
    You see, our numbers could with ease compel
    What we request. And what do we request?
    Only to save yourselves?

The Women *with their children gathering about the* Men.

OROONOKO.   I'll hear no more.

WOMEN.

    Hear him, hear him. He takes no care of us.   50

GOVERNOR.

    To those poor wretches who have been seduced
    And led away, to all and everyone,
    We offer a full pardon—

OROONOKO.   Then fall on.

                             Preparing to engage.

GOVERNOR.

    Lay hold upon't before it be too late,
    Pardon and mercy.

The Women *clinging about the* Men, *they leave* Oroonoko *and fall upon their faces crying out for pardon.*

SLAVES.   Pardon, mercy, pardon.   55

OROONOKO.

    Let 'em go all. Now, Governor, I see,
    I own the folly of my enterprise,
    The rashness of this action, and must blush
    Quite through this veil of night, a whitely shame,
    To think I could design to make those free   60
    Who were by nature slaves—wretches designed

40. Resolved!] Resolved, *all edns.*

To be their masters' dogs and lick their feet.
Whip, whip 'em to the knowledge of your gods,
Your Christian gods, who suffer you to be
Unjust, dishonest, cowardly, and base,   65
And give 'em your excuse for being so.
I would not live on the same earth with creatures
That only have the faces of their kind.
Why should they look like men who are not so?
When they put off their noble natures for   70
The grovelling qualities of downcast beasts,
I wish they had their tails.

ABOAN.   Then we should know 'em.

OROONOKO (*to* Imoinda, Aboan).
We were too few before for victory;
We're still enow to die.

                    Blanford *enters.*

GOVERNOR.   Live, royal sir,
Live and be happy long on your own terms;   75
Only consent to yield, and you shall have
What terms you can propose for you and yours.

OROONOKO.
Consent to yield! Shall I betray myself?

GOVERNOR.
Alas! We cannot fear that your small force,
The force of two, with a weak woman's arm,   80
Should conquer us. I speak in the regard
And honor of your worth, in my desire
And forwardness to serve so great a man.
I would not have it lie upon my thoughts
That I was the occasion of the fall   85
Of such a prince, whose courage carried on
In a more noble cause would well deserve
The empire of the world.

OROONOKO.   You can speak fair.

---

64. *Christian gods*] Southerne tones down Behn's hero's attack on
the perfidy of Christians and on Christianity. Compare Behn, 5: 196.

GOVERNOR.

    Your undertaking, though it would have brought
    So great a loss to us, we must all say					90
    Was generous and noble and shall be
    Regarded only as the fire of youth
    That will break out sometimes in gallant souls.
    We'll think it but the natural impulse,
    A rash impatience of liberty,					95
    No otherwise.

OROONOKO.   Think it what you will.

    I was not born to render an account
    Of what I do to any but myself.

            Blanford *comes forward.*

BLANFORD *(to the* Governor).

    I'm glad you have proceeded by fair means.
    I came to be a mediator.					100

GOVERNOR.

    Try what you can work upon him.

OROONOKO.

    Are you come against me too?

BLANFORD.

    Is this to come against you?   *Offering his sword to* Oroonoko.
    Unarmed to put myself into your hands?
    I come, I hope, to serve you.

OROONOKO. You have served me;					105
    I thank you for't. And I am pleased to think
    You were my friend while I had need of one.
    But now 'tis past; this farewell, and be gone.   *Embraces him.*

BLANFORD.

    It is not past, and I must serve you still.
    I would make up these breaches which the sword					110
    Will widen more and close us all in love.

OROONOKO.

    I know what I have done and I should be
    A child to think they ever can forgive.

93. gallant souls] *Q3, H, C1–2,
S;* gallant so[ ] *Q1;* gallant; so
Q2.

Forgive! Were there but that, I would not live
To be forgiven. Is there a power on earth   115
That I can ever need forgiveness from?

BLANFORD.
You sha'not need it.

OROONOKO.   No, I wonnot need it.

BLANFORD.
You see he offers you your own conditions
For you and yours.

OROONOKO.   I must capitulate?
Precariously compound on stinted terms   120
To save my life?

BLANFORD.   Sir, he imposes none.
You make 'em for your own security.
If your great heart cannot descend to treat
In adverse fortune with an enemy,
Yet sure, your honor's safe, you may accept   125
Offers of peace and safety from a friend.

GOVERNOR (to Blanford).
He will rely on what you say to him.
Offer him what you can; I will confirm
And make all good. Be you my pledge of trust.

BLANFORD.
I'll answer with my life for all he says.   130

GOVERNOR (aside).
Ay, do, and pay the forfeit if you please.

BLANFORD (of Imoinda).
Consider, sir, can you consent to throw
That blessing from you, you so hardly found
And so much valued once?

OROONOKO.   Imoinda! O!
'Tis she that holds me on this argument   135
Of tedious life. I could resolve it soon
Were this curst being only in debate.
But my Imoinda struggles in my soul.
She makes a coward of me. I confess
I am afraid to part with her in death   140
And more afraid of life to lose her here.

Sexism

BLANFORD.

    This way you must lose her; think upon
    The weakness of her sex, made yet more weak
    With her condition, requiring rest
    And soft indulging ease, to nurse your hopes   145
    And make you a glad father.

OROONOKO.   There I feel

    A father's fondness and a husband's love.
    They seize upon my heart, strain all its strings
    To pull me to 'em from my stern resolve.
    Husband and father! All the melting art   150
    Of eloquence lives in those soft'ning names.
    Methinks I see the babe with infant hands
    Pleading for life and begging to be born.
    Shall I forbid his birth? Deny him light?
    The heavenly comforts of all cheering light?   155
    And make the womb the dungeon of his death?
    His bleeding mother his sad monument?
    These are the calls of nature that call loud;
    They will be heard and conquer in their cause.
    He must not be a man who can resist 'em.   160
    No, my Imoinda! I will venture all
    To save thee and that little innocent.
    The world may be a better friend to him
    Than I have found it. Now I yield myself.

                          Gives up his sword.

    The conflict's past, and we are in your hands.   165

    Several men get about Oroonoko *and* Aboan *and seize 'em.*

GOVERNOR.

    So you shall find you are. Dispose of them
    As I commanded you.

BLANFORD.   Good heav'n forbid!

    You cannot mean—

---

    147. *father's fondness*] This passage concerning Imoinda's "condition" and Oroonoko's fatherly instincts provides a softening of his character that is not in Southerne's source (Behn, 5: 196).

    164. *yield myself*] Behn's Oroonoko demands a written surrender agreement, which Governor Byam nevertheless violates immediately. Southerne tries to maintain Oroonoko's sense of dignity and his trust in Blanford.

GOVERNOR (*to* Blanford *who goes to* Oroonoko).
                    This is not your concern.
    (*To* Imoinda.) I must take care of you.
IMOINDA.   I'm at the end
    Of all my care; here I will die with him.   170
                                    Holding Oroonoko.

OROONOKO.
    You shall not force her from me.   *He holds her.*
GOVERNOR.   Then I must
    Try other means and conquer force by force.
    Break, cut off his hold, bring her away.
                                They force her from him.

IMOINDA.
    I do not ask to live; kill me but here.
OROONOKO.
    O bloody dogs! Inhuman murderers!   175

Imoinda *forced out of one door by the* Governor *and others.*
Oroonoko *and* Aboan *hurried out of another.*   *Exeunt omnes.*

175. Inhuman] *Q2, C1–2, S;* In-
humane *Q1, H;* In humane *Q3.*

ACT V

[V.i]   *Enter* Stanmore, Lucy, Charlotte.

STANMORE.

'Tis strange we cannot hear of him. Can nobody give an
account of him?

LUCY.

Nay, I begin to despair; I give him for gone.

STANMORE.

Not so I hope.

LUCY.

There are so many disturbances in this devilish country!   5
Would we had never seen it.

STANMORE.

This is but a cold welcome for you, madam, after so
troublesome a voyage.

CHARLOTTE.

A cold welcome indeed, sir, without my cousin Welldon;
he was the best friend I had in the world.   10

STANMORE.

He was a very good friend of yours indeed, madam.

LUCY.

They have made him away, murdered him for his money,
I believe; he took a considerable sum out with him, I
know. That has been his ruin.

STANMORE.

That has done him no injury to my knowledge, for this   15
morning he put into my custody what you speak of, I
suppose a thousand pounds, for the use of this lady.

CHARLOTTE.

I was always obliged to him, and he has shown his care
of me in placing my little affairs in such honorable hands.

14. know.] know, *Q1–3, H, C1–2;*
know *S.*

— 96 —

STANMORE.

He gave me a particular charge of you, madam, very 20
particular, so particular that you will be surprised when
I tell you.

CHARLOTTE.

What, pray sir?

STANMORE.

I am engaged to get you a husband; I promised that
before I saw you, and now I have seen you, you must 25
give me leave to offer you myself.

LUCY.

Nay, cousin, never be coy upon the matter; to my knowledge my brother always designed you for this gentleman.

STANMORE.

You hear, madam, he has given me his interest, and 'tis
the favor I would have begged of him. Lord! You are 30
so like him—

CHARLOTTE.

That you are obliged to say you like me for his sake.

STANMORE.

I should be glad to love you for your own.

CHARLOTTE.

If I should consent to the fine things you can say to
me, how would you look at last to find 'em thrown 35
away upon an old acquaintance?

STANMORE.

An old acquaintance!

CHARLOTTE.

Lord, how easily are you men to be imposed upon! I am
no cousin newly arrived from England, not I, but the
very Welldon you wot of.   40

STANMORE.

Welldon!

CHARLOTTE.

Not murdered nor made away, as my sister would have

23. sir?] *H, C1–2, S;* sir *Q1–3.*   41. Welldon!] *Q1–3, C1–2, S;*
33. to] *Q1–3, C1–2, S;* ro *H.*   Welldon? *H.*
36. acquaintance?] *Q1–2, S;* acquaintance! *Q3, H, C1–2.*

you believe, but am in very good health, your old friend in breeches that was and now your humble servant in petticoats.   45

STANMORE.

I'm glad we have you again. But what service can you do me in petticoats, pray?

CHARLOTTE.

Can't you tell what?

STANMORE.

Not I, by my troth. I have found my friend and lost my mistress, it seems, which I did not expect from your   50 petticoats.

CHARLOTTE.

Come, come, you have had a friend of your mistress long enough; 'tis high time now to have a mistress of your friend.

STANMORE.

What do you say?   55

CHARLOTTE.

I am a woman, sir.

STANMORE.

A woman!

CHARLOTTE.

As arrant a woman as you would have had me but now, I assure you.

STANMORE.

And at my service?   60

CHARLOTTE.

If you have any for me in petticoats.

STANMORE.

Yes, yes, I shall find you employment.

CHARLOTTE.

You wonder at my proceeding, I believe.

STANMORE.

'Tis a little extraordinary, indeed.

CHARLOTTE.

I have taken some pains to come into your favor.   65

58. me but] *H, C1–2, S;* me. But *Q1–3.*

STANMORE.

You might have had it cheaper a great deal.

CHARLOTTE.

I might have married you in the person of my English cousin, but could not consent to cheat you even in the thing I had a mind to.

STANMORE.

'Twas done as you do everything.   70

CHARLOTTE.

I need not tell you I made that little plot and carried it on only for this opportunity. I was resolved to see whether you liked me as a woman or not. If I had found you indifferent, I would have endeavored to have been so too; but you say you like me, and therefore I have   75 ventured to discover the truth.

STANMORE.

Like you! I like you so well that I'm afraid you won't think marriage a proof on't. Shall I give you any other?

CHARLOTTE.

No, no, I'm inclined to believe you, and that shall convince me. At more leisure I'll satisfy you how I came to   80 be in man's clothes, for no ill I assure you, though I have happened to play the rogue in 'em. They have assisted me in marrying my sister and have gone a great way in befriending your cousin Jack with the widow. Can you forgive me for pimping for your family?   85

Enter Jack Stanmore.

STANMORE.

So, Jack, what news with you?

JACK STANMORE.

I am the forepart of the widow, you know; she's coming after with the body of the family, the young squire in her hand, my son-in-law that is to be with the help of Mr. Welldon.   90

---

87. *forepart*] advance guard; but also with its possible meaning of "stomacher," an ornamental breast covering for a woman, and therefore sexual in implication.

CHARLOTTE (*clapping* Jack *upon the back*).
Say you so, sir?

Enter Widow Lackitt *with her son* Daniel.

WIDOW.

So, Mrs. Lucy, I have brought him about again. I have
chastised him; I have made him as supple as a glove
for your wearing to pull on or throw off at your pleasure.
Will you ever rebel again? Will you, sirrah? But come,   95
come, down on your marrow bones and ask her forgiveness. Say after me, pray forsooth wife.   Daniel *kneels*.

DANIEL.

Pray forsooth wife.

LUCY.

Well, well, this is a day of good nature, and so I take
you into favor. But first take the oath of allegiance. 100
If ever you do so again—

He kisses her hand and rises.

DANIEL.

Nay, marry if I do, I shall have the worst on't.

LUCY.

Here's a stranger, forsooth, would be glad to be known
to you, a sister of mine; pray salute her.

WIDOW (*starts at* Charlotte).

Your sister! Mrs. Lucy! What do you mean? This is your 105
brother, Mr. Welldon; do you think I do not know Mr.
Welldon?

LUCY.

Have a care what you say. This gentleman's about marrying her. You may spoil all.

WIDOW.

Fiddle faddle, what! You would put a trick upon me.   110

CHARLOTTE.

No, faith, Widow, the trick is over; it has taken suffi-

---

100. *oath of allegiance*] The new oaths of allegiance established by
the Convention Parliament in 1689 required all office holders to
acknowledge the sovereignty of William and Mary. Lucy is here setting herself up as Daniel's "lord and master."

ciently, and now I will teach you the trick to prevent
your being cheated another time.

WIDOW.

How! Cheated, Mr. Welldon!

CHARLOTTE.

Why, ay, you will always take things by the wrong 115
handle. I see you will have me Mr. Welldon. I grant
you I was Mr. Welldon a little while to please you or
so, but Mr. Stanmore here has persuaded me into a
woman again.

WIDOW.

A woman! Pray let me speak with you. (*Drawing her* 120
aside.) You are not in earnest, I hope? A woman!

CHARLOTTE.

Really a woman.

WIDOW.

Gads my life! I could not be cheated in everything. I
know a man from a woman at these years, or the devil's
in't. Pray, did not you marry me?   125

CHARLOTTE.

You would have it so.

WIDOW.

And did not I give you a thousand pounds this morning?

CHARLOTTE.

Yes indeed, 'twas more than I deserved, but you had your
penniworth for your penny, I suppose. You seemed to
be pleased with your bargain.   130

WIDOW.

A rare bargain I have made on't, truly. I have laid out
my money to fine purpose upon a woman.

CHARLOTTE.

You would have a husband, and I provided for you as
well as I could.

WIDOW.

Yes, yes, you have provided for me.   135

CHARLOTTE.

And you have paid me very well for't, I thank you.

WIDOW.

'Tis very well; I may be with child too for aught I know
and may go look for the father.

CHARLOTTE.

Nay, if you think so, 'tis time to look about you indeed.
Ev'n make up the matter as well as you can, I advise you 140
as a friend, and let us live neighborly and lovingly
together.

WIDOW.

I have nothing else for it that I know now.

CHARLOTTE.

For my part, Mrs. Lackitt, your thousand pounds will
engage me not to laugh at you. Then my sister is mar- 145
ried to your son; he is to have half your estate, I know.
And indeed they may live upon it very comfortably to
themselves and very creditably to you.

WIDOW.

Nay, I can blame nobody but myself.

CHARLOTTE.

You have enough for a husband still, and that you may 150
bestow upon honest Jack Stanmore.

WIDOW.

Is he the man then?

CHARLOTTE.

He is the man you are obliged to.

JACK STANMORE.

Yes, faith, Widow, I am the man. I have done fairly by
you, you find; you know what you have to trust to 155
beforehand.

WIDOW.

Well, well, I see you will have me. Ev'n marry me and
make an end of the business.

STANMORE.

Why, that's well said; now we are all agreed and all
provided for.   160

A Servant *enters to* Stanmore.

SERVANT.

Sir, Mr. Blanford desires you to come to him and bring
as many of your friends as you can with you.

STANMORE.

I come to him. You'll all go along with me. Come,

young gentleman, marriage is the fashion, you see; you
must like it now.   165

DANIEL.

If I don't, how shall I help myself?

LUCY.

Nay, you may hang yourself in the noose, if you please,
but you'll never get out on't with struggling.

DANIEL.

Come then, let's ev'n jog on in the old road.
Cuckold or worse, I must be now contented.   170
I'm not the first has married and repented.   *Exeunt.*

[V.ii]   *Enter* Governor *with* Blanford *and* Planters.

BLANFORD.

Have you no reverence of future fame?
No awe upon your actions from the tongues,
The censuring tongues of men that will be free?
If you confess humanity, believe
There is a God, or devil, to reward   5
Our doings here, do not provoke your fate.
The hand of Heaven is armed against these crimes
With hotter thunderbolts prepared to shoot
And nail you to the earth a sad example,
A monument of faithless infamy.   10

Enter Stanmore, Jack Stanmore, Charlotte, Lucy, Widow, *and*
Daniel.

So, Stanmore, you, I know, the women too,
Will join with me.
      (*To the women.*) 'Tis Oroonoko's cause,
A lover's cause, a wretched woman's cause,
That will become your intercession.

1 PLANTER.

Never mind 'em, Governor; he ought to be made an   15
example for the good of the plantation.

---

171. *married and repented*] an echo of the proverb, "Marry today,
repent tomorrow" (Tilley, M 694).

2 PLANTER.

Ay, ay, 'twill frighten the Negroes from attempting the like again.

1 PLANTER.

What! Rise against their lords and masters! At this rate no man is safe from his own slaves.   20

2 PLANTER.

No, no more he is. Therefore, one and all, Governor, we declare for hanging.

OMNES PLANTERS.

Ay, ay, hang him, hang him.

WIDOW.

What! Hang him! O! Forbid it, Governor.

CHARLOTTE. LUCY.

We all petition for him.   25

JACK STANMORE.

They are for a holiday; guilty or not is not the business. Hanging is their sport.

BLANFORD.

We are not sure so wretched to have these,
The rabble, judge for us; the changing crowd,
The arbitrary guard of fortune's power,   30
Who wait to catch the sentence of her frowns
And hurry all to ruin she condemns.

STANMORE.

So far from farther wrong that 'tis a shame
He should be where he is. Good Governor,
Order his liberty. He yielded up   35
Himself, his all, at your discretion.

BLANFORD.

Discretion! No, he yielded on your word;

19. What!] *Q1, Q3;* What, *Q2,*   26. holiday] *C1-2, S;* holy day
H, C1-2, S.   *Q1-3, H.*

---

29. *The rabble*] Southerne specialized in scenes such as these in which the stupidity of the mob was revealed, but although the tone is pure Southerne, the material is present in Behn, who informs us that the Council "consisted of such notorious Villains as *Newgate* never transported; and, possibly, originally were such who understood neither the Laws of God or Man" (Behn, 5: 200).

And I am made the cautionary pledge,
The gage and hostage of your keeping it.
Remember, sir, he yielded on your word.   40
Your word! Which honest men will think should be
The last resort of truth and trust on earth.
There's no appeal beyond it but to Heav'n.
An oath is a recognizance to Heav'n,
Binding us over in the courts above   45
To plead to the indictment of our crimes,
That those who 'scape this world should suffer there.
But in the common intercourse of men
(Where the dread majesty is not invoked,
His honor not immediately concerned,   50
Not made a party in our interests),
Our word is all to be relied upon.

WIDOW.
Come, come, you'll be as good as your word, we know.

STANMORE.
He's out of all power of doing any harm now, if he were
disposed to it.   55

CHARLOTTE.
But he is not disposed to it.

BLANFORD.
To keep him where he is will make him soon
Find out some desperate way to liberty.
He'll hang himself or dash out his mad brains.

CHARLOTTE.
Pray try him by gentle means. We'll all be sureties for   60
him.

OMNES.
All, all.

LUCY.
We will all answer for him now.

46. plead to the] *Q1, Q3, H,*
C1–2, S; plead the *Q2*

GOVERNOR.

    Well, you will have it so, do what you please, just what
    you will with him, I give you leave.   *Exit.* 65

BLANFORD.

    We thank you, sir; this way, pray come with me.   *Exeunt.*

[V.iii] *The scene drawn shows* Oroonoko *upon his back, his
legs and arms stretched out, and chained to the ground. Enter*
Blanford, Stanmore, [Widow Lackitt, Charlotte] *and others.*

BLANFORD.

    O miserable sight! Help everyone,
    Assist me all to free him from his chains.

    They help him up and bring him forward, looking down.

    Most injured prince! How shall we clear ourselves?
    We cannot hope you will vouchsafe to hear
    Or credit what we say in the defense   5
    And cause of our suspected innocence.

STANMORE.

    We are not guilty of your injuries,
    No way consenting to 'em, but abhor,
    Abominate, and loathe this cruelty.

BLANFORD.

    It is our curse, but make it not our crime,   10
    A heavy curse upon us that we must
    Share anything in common, ev'n the light,
    The elements, and seasons with such men,
    Whose principles, like the famed dragon's teeth,

---

    65. *give you leave*] In Behn's *Oroonoko*, Trefry simply argues that
Byam's power as Lieutenant-Governor did not extend to Parham,
which was the property of the Governor, and hence a sanctuary
(Behn, 5: 200).

    14. *dragon's teeth*] Cadmus, the brother of Europa, followed the
commands of the Delphic oracle and came to a spring where he was
to make a sacrifice. His companions were slain by a dragon who was
guarding the spring, and after killing the dragon, Cadmus was
ordered by Athena to sow the dragon's teeth in the ground. As soon
as the teeth were sown a host of armed men sprang up and fought
among themselves. With the five survivors, Cadmus founded the
Cadmea, the stronghold of Thebes.

Scattered and sown, would shoot a harvest up   15
Of fighting mischiefs to confound themselves
And ruin all about 'em.
STANMORE.   Profligates!
Whose bold Titanian impiety
Would once again pollute their mother earth,
Force her to teem with her old monstrous brood   20
Of giants and forget the race of men.
BLANFORD.
We are not so; believe us innocent.
We come prepared with all our services
To offer a redress of your base wrongs.
Which way shall we employ 'em?
STANMORE.   Tell us, sir.   25
If there is anything that can atone;
But nothing can that may be some amends—
OROONOKO.
If you would have me think you are not all
Confederates, all accessory to
The base injustice of your governor;   30
If you would have me live, as you appear
Concerned for me; if you would have me live
To thank and bless you, there is yet a way
To tie me ever to your honest love.
Bring my Imoinda to me; give me her   35
To charm my sorrows, and, if possible,
I'll sit down with my wrongs, never to rise
Against my fate or think of vengeance more.
BLANFORD.
Be satisfied, you may depend upon us;
We'll bring her safe to you and suddenly.   40
CHARLOTTE.
We wonnot leave you in so good a work.

---

18. *Titanian impiety*] The Titans ruled by Chronus were defeated
by Zeus and the gods of Olympus and imprisoned below Tartarus.

21. *giants*] This is probably a reference to the *gigantes,* who, led
by Alcyoneus, Porphyrion, and Enceladus, waged war with the gods,
hurling rocks and burning tree trunks at heaven. Their revolt is
often mingled with the wars of the gods and the Titans.

WIDOW.
     No, no, we'll go with you.
BLANFORD.   In the meantime
     Endeavor to forget, sir, and forgive,
     And hope a better fortune.   *Exeunt.*
OROONOKO (*alone*).
     Forget! Forgive! I must indeed forget   45
     When I forgive; but while I am a man
     In flesh that bears the living mark of shame,
     The print of his dishonorable chains,
     My memory still rousing up my wrongs,
     I never can forgive this governor,   50
     This villain: the disgrace of trust and place
     And just contempt of delegated power.
     What shall I do? If I declare myself,
     I know him, he will sneak behind his guard
     Of followers and brave me in his fears.   55
     Else, lion-like, with my devouring rage,
     I would rush on him, fasten on his throat,
     Tear wide a passage to his treacherous heart,
     And that way lay him open to the world.   *Pausing.*
     If I should turn his Christian arts on him,   60
     Promise him, speak him fair, flatter, and creep
     With fawning steps to get within his faith,
     I could betray him then as he has me.
     But am I sure by that to right myself?
     Lying's a certain mark of cowardice;   65
     And when the tongue forgets its honesty,
     The heart and hand may drop their functions too
     And nothing worthy be resolved or done.
     The man must go together, bad or good:
     In one part frail, he soon grows weak in all.   70
     Honor should be concerned in honor's cause;
     That is not to be cured by contraries

71. cause] cause, *all edns.*

---

55. *brave*] defy.
72. *That*] i.e., Honor.
72. *contraries*] qualities which are absolutely different and destroy
one another. Theophrastus Paracelsus and his followers, for example,

As bodies are whose health is often drawn
From rankest poisons. Let me but find out
An honest remedy; I have the hand,   75
A minist'ring hand, that will apply it home.   *Exit.*

[V.iv]   *The Governor's house. Enter* Governor.

GOVERNOR.
I would not have her tell me she consents:
In favor of the sex's modesty
That still should be presumed, because there is
A greater impudence in owning it
Than in allowing all that we can do.   5
This truth I know, and yet against myself
(So unaccountable are lovers' ways)
I talk and lose the opportunities
Which love and she expects I should employ.
Ev'n she expects, for when a man has said   10
All that is fit to save the decency,
The women know the rest is to be done.
I wonnot disappoint her.   *Going.*

---

advised curing "a hot and dry disease" with a fluid and drying up
a "humid disease." See Paracelsus, *Medicina Diastatica*, ed. Andrea
Tentzelius, trans. Ferdinando Parkhurst (London, 1653), p. 70.

74. *rankest poisons*] Opium, for example, was classified as a poison,
though its potential curative use was known. See W[illiam] R[amesey].
Lifes Security (London, 1665), pp. 94–96; Richard Mead, *A Mechanical
Account of Poisons* (London, 1702). pp. 131–48.

76. *minist'ring*] administering, in the sense of administering medi-
cines with an implied sense of administering justice.

1. *she consents*] In Behn's *Oroonoko* Imoinda is admired by Trefry,
but he is pleased to find that she is Oroonoko's lost love. The Governor's passion for her is Southerne's invention. Behn's Imoinda is
also in an advanced stage of pregnancy at this point in the story
(Behn, 5: 173–74).

1–13. *I . . . her.*] The Governor is here making a cynical distinction
between Imoinda's telling him she consents and her allowing him
sexual liberties. His torturous syntax parallels the involution of his
rationalizations about Imoinda's affections and his own worldly attitude
toward women and their necessary pretense where reputation is concerned.

Enter to him Blanford, *the* Stanmores, Daniel, Mrs. Lackitt,
Charlotte, *and* Lucy.

WIDOW.

O Governor! I'm glad we have lit upon you.

GOVERNOR.

Why! What's the matter?   15

CHARLOTTE.

Nay, nothing extraordinary. But one good action draws
on another. You have given the prince his freedom; now
we come a-begging for his wife. You won't refuse us.

GOVERNOR.

Refuse you! No, no, what have I to do to refuse you?

WIDOW.

You won't refuse to send her to him, she means.   20

GOVERNOR.

I send her to him!

WIDOW.

We have promised him to bring her.

GOVERNOR.

You do very well; 'tis kindly done of you. Ev'n carry
her to him with all my heart.

LUCY.

You must tell us where she is.   25

GOVERNOR.

I tell you! Why, don't you know?

BLANFORD.

Your servants say she's in the house.

GOVERNOR.

No, no, I brought her home at first indeed; but I thought
it would not look well to keep her here. I removed her
in the hurry only to take care of her. What! She belongs   30
to you. I have nothing to do with her.

CHARLOTTE.

But where is she now, sir?

GOVERNOR.

Why, faith, I can't say certainly. You'll hear of her at

— 110 —

Parham House, I suppose, there or thereabouts, I think
I sent her there.   35
BLANFORD (*aside*).
    I'll have an eye on him.   *Exeunt all but the* Governor.
GOVERNOR.
    I have lied myself into a little time
    And must employ it. They'll be here again,
    But I must be before 'em.
                    Going out, he meets Imoinda *and seizes her.*
                    Are you come!
    I'll court no longer for a happiness   40
    That is in mine own keeping; you may still
    Refuse to grant, so I have power to take.
    The man that asks deserves to be denied.

*She disengages one hand and draws his sword from his side upon
him.* Governor *starts and retires;* Blanford *enters behind him.*

IMOINDA.
    He does indeed that asks unworthily.
BLANFORD.
    You hear her, sir, that asks unworthily.   45
GOVERNOR.
    You are no judge.
BLANFORD.   I am of my own slave.
GOVERNOR.
    Begone and leave us.
BLANFORD.   When you let her go.
GOVERNOR.
    To fasten upon you.
BLANFORD.   I must defend myself.
IMOINDA.
    Help, murder, help!

Imoinda *retreats towards the door favored by* Blanford; *when
they are closed, she throws down the sword and runs out.* Gov-

34. *Parham House*] The Governor's mansion was named after Lord
Willoughby, Earl of Parham, who founded the first permanent colony.
See John Stedman, *Expedition to Surinam,* ed. Christopher Briant
(London, 1963), p. v.

ernor *takes up the sword; they fight, close, and fall,* Blanford
upon him. Servants enter and part 'em.

GOVERNOR.

    She shannot 'scape me so. I've gone too far   50
    Not to go farther. Curse on my delay;
    But yet she is and shall be in my power.

BLANFORD.

    Nay, then it is the war of honesty;
    I know you and will save you from yourself.

GOVERNOR.

    All come along with me.   *Exeunt.* 55

[V.v]   Oroonoko *enters.*

OROONOKO.

    To honor bound! And yet a slave to love!
    I am distracted by their rival powers,
    And both will be obeyed. O great revenge!
    Thou raiser and restorer of fall'n fame!
    Let me not be unworthy of thy aid   5
    For stopping in thy course. I still am thine,
    But can't forget I am Imoinda's too;
    She calls me from my wrongs to rescue her.
    No man condemn me who has never felt
    A woman's power or tried the force of love. 10
    All tempers yield and soften in those fires.
    Our honors, interests resolving down,
    Run in the gentle current of our joys,
    But not to sink and drown our memory.
    We mount again to action like the sun   15
    That rises from the bosom of the sea
    To run his glorious race of light anew
    And carry on the world. Love, love will be
    My first ambition, and my fame the next.

           Aboan *enters bloody.*

    My eyes are turned against me and combine 20

3. be] *Q1–2, H, C1–2, S;* om.
Q3.

With my sworn enemies to represent
This spectacle of honor. Aboan!
My ever faithful friend!

ABOAN.   I have no name
That can distinguish me from the vile earth
To which I'm going: a poor, abject worm   25
That crawled awhile upon a bustling world
And now am trampled to my dust again.

OROONOKO.
I see thee gashed and mangled.

ABOAN.   Spare my shame
To tell how they have used me; but believe
The hangman's hand would have been merciful.   30
Do not you scorn me, sir, to think I can
Intend to live under this infamy.
I do not come for pity to complain.
I've spent an honorable life with you,
The earliest servant of your rising fame,   35
And would attend it with my latest care.
My life was yours and so shall be my death.
You must not live—
Bending and sinking, I have dragged my steps
Thus far to tell you that you cannot live,   40
To warn you of those ignominious wrongs,
Whips, rods, and all the instruments of death
Which I have felt and are prepared for you.
This was the duty that I had to pay.
'Tis done, and now I beg to be discharged.   45

OROONOKO.
What shall I do for thee?

22. honor] honour *Q1–3, H,
C1–2;* horror *S (see expl. note below).*

---

22. *honor*] Many later editions and versions of the play accept the
S reading of "horror" for "honor", among them are the following:
Dublin, 1731; Hawkesworth revision, 1759; anonymous revision, 1760;
Gentleman revision, 1760 (see Introduction, pp. xix–xx). Inchbald
omits the entire sentence.

ABOAN.   My body tires
      And wonnot bear me off to liberty;
      I shall again be taken, made a slave.
      A sword, a dagger yet would rescue me.
      I have not strength to go to find out death.   50
      You must direct him to me.
OROONOKO.   Here he is,

                                        Gives him a dagger.

      The only present I can make thee now,
      And next the honorable means of life,
      I would bestow the honest means of death.
ABOAN.

      I cannot stay to thank you. If there is   55
      A being after this, I shall be yours
      In the next world, your faithful slave again.
      This is to try.   *Stabs himself.*
                        I had a living sense
      Of all your royal favors, but this last
      Strikes through my heart. I wonnot say farewell,   60
      For you must follow me.   *Dies.*
OROONOKO.   In life and death
      The guardian of my honor! Follow thee!
      I should have gone before thee; then perhaps
      Thy fate had been prevented. All his care
      Was to preserve me from the barbarous rage   65
      That wronged him only for being mine.
      Why, why, you gods! Why am I so accurst
      That it must be a reason of your wrath,
      A guilt, a crime sufficient to the fate
      Of anyone, but to belong to me?   70
      My friend has found it and my wife will soon.
      My wife! The very fear's too much for life;
      I can't support it. Where? Imoinda! O!

          Going out, she meets him, running into his arms.

      Thou bosom softness! Down of all my cares!

71. My] *Q2–3, H, C1–2, S;* Ny   74. softness] *Q2–3, H, C1–2, S;*
Q1.   sotfness *Q1.*

───────────────────────────────

I could recline my thoughts upon this breast   75
To a forgetfulness of all my griefs
And yet be happy, but it wonnot be.
Thou art disordered, pale, and out of breath!
If fate pursues thee, find a shelter here.
What is it thou wouldst tell me?

IMOINDA.   'Tis in vain   80
To call him villain.

OROONOKO.   Call him Governor.
Is it not so?

IMOINDA.   There's not another sure.

OROONOKO.
Villain's the common name of mankind here,
But his most properly. What! What of him?
I fear to be resolved and must enquire.   85
He had thee in his power.

IMOINDA.   I blush to think it.

OROONOKO.
Blush! To think what?

IMOINDA.   That I was in his power.

OROONOKO.
He could not use it?

IMOINDA.   What can't such men do?

OROONOKO.
But did he? Durst he?

IMOINDA.   What he could, he dared.

OROONOKO.
His own gods damn him then! For ours have none,   90
No punishment for such unheard-of crimes.

IMOINDA.
This monster, cunning in his flatteries,
When he had wearied all his useless arts,
Leapt out, fierce as a beast of prey, to seize me.
I trembled, feared.

OROONOKO.   I fear and tremble now.   95
What could preserve thee? What deliver thee?

IMOINDA.
That worthy man you used to call your friend—

OROONOKO.
Blanford.

IMOINDA.			Came in and saved me from his rage.

OROONOKO.

He was a friend indeed to rescue thee!
And for his sake I'll think it possible					100
A Christian may be yet an honest man.

IMOINDA.

O! Did you know what I have struggled through
To save me yours, sure you would promise me
Never to see me forced from you again.

OROONOKO.

To promise thee! O! Do I need to promise?					105
But there is now no farther use of words.
Death is security for all our fears.

> *Shows Aboan's body on the floor.*

And yet I cannot trust him.

IMOINDA.						Aboan!

OROONOKO.

Mangled and torn, resolved to give me time
To fit myself for what I must expect,					110
Groaned out a warning to me and expired.

IMOINDA.

For what you must expect?

OROONOKO.						Would that were all.

IMOINDA.

What! To be butchered thus—

OROONOKO.						Just as thou see'st.

IMOINDA.

By barbarous hands, to fall at last their prey!

OROONOKO.

I have run the race with honor; shall I now					115
Lag and be overtaken at the goal?

IMOINDA.						No.

OROONOKO (*tenderly*).

I must look back to thee.

IMOINDA.						You shannot need.

I'm always present to your purpose; say
Which way would you dispose me?

OROONOKO.						Have a care,

Thou'rt on a precipice and dost not see					120
Whither that question leads thee. O! Too soon

Thou dost enquire what the assembled gods
Have not determined and will latest doom.
Yet this I know of fate, this is most certain:
I cannot as I would dispose of thee;   125
And as I ought I dare not. O Imoinda!

IMOINDA.

Alas! That sigh! Why do you tremble so?
Nay, then 'tis bad indeed if you can weep.

OROONOKO.

My heart runs over; if my gushing eyes
Betray a weakness which they never knew,   130
Believe thou, only thou couldst cause these tears.
The gods themselves conspire with faithless men
To our destruction.

IMOINDA.   Heav'n and earth our foes!

OROONOKO.

It is not always granted to the great
To be most happy. If the angry pow'rs   135
Repent their favors, let 'em take 'em back.
The hopes of empire which they gave my youth
By making me a prince I here resign.
Let 'em quench in me all those glorious fires
Which kindled at their beams; that lust of fame,   140
That fever of ambition, restless still
And burning with the sacred thirst of sway
Which they inspired to qualify my fate
And make me fit to govern under them,
Let 'em extinguish. I submit myself   145
To their high pleasure and devoted bow
Yet lower to continue still a slave
Hopeless of liberty; and if I could
Live after it, would give up honor too
To satisfy their vengeance, to avert   150
This only curse, the curse of losing thee.

IMOINDA.

If Heav'n could be appeased, these cruel men

128. Nay,] S; Nay Q1–3, C1–2,
H.

Are not to be entreated or believed.
O! Think on that and be no more deceived.
OROONOKO.
    What can we do?
IMOINDA.   Can I do anything?   155
OROONOKO.
    But we were born to suffer.
IMOINDA.   Suffer both,
    Both die, and so prevent 'em.
OROONOKO.   By thy death!
    O! Let me hunt my travelled thoughts again,
    Range the wide waste of desolate despair,
    Start any hope. Alas! I lose myself;   160
    'Tis pathless, dark, and barren all to me.
    Thou art my only guide, my light of life,
    And thou art leaving me. Send out thy beams
    Upon the wing; let 'em fly all around,
    Discover every way. Is there a dawn,   165
    A glimmering of comfort? The great god
    That rises on the world must shine on us.
IMOINDA.
    And see us set before him.
OROONOKO.   Thou bespeak'st
    And go'st before me.
IMOINDA.   So I would, in love:
    In the dear unsuspected part of life,   170
    In death for love. Alas! What hopes for me?
    I was preserved but to acquit myself,
    To beg to die with you.
OROONOKO.   And can'st thou ask it?
    I never durst enquire into myself
    About thy fate, and thou resolv'st it all.   175
IMOINDA.
    Alas! My lord! My fate's resolved in yours.
OROONOKO.
    O! Keep thee there. Let not thy virtue shrink

169. go'st] goest *H, C1–2, S;*
goes *Q1–3.*

From my support, and I will gather strength
Fast as I can to tell thee—
IMOINDA.   I must die.
I know 'tis fit and I can die with you.   180
OROONOKO.
O! Thou hast banished hence a thousand fears
Which sickened at my heart and quite unmanned me.
IMOINDA.
Your fear's for me; I know you feared my strength
And could not overcome your tenderness
To pass this sentence on me. And indeed   185
There you were kind, as I have always found you,
As you have ever been; for though I am
Resigned and ready to obey my doom,
Methinks it should not be pronounced by you.
OROONOKO.
O! That was all the labor of my grief.   190
My heart and tongue forsook me in the strife.
I never could pronounce it.
IMOINDA.
I have for you, for both of us.
OROONOKO.
Alas! For me! My death
I could regard as the last scene of life   195
And act it through with joy to have it done.
But then to part with thee—
IMOINDA.   'Tis hard to part.
But parting thus, as the most happy must,
Parting in death, makes it the easier.
You might have thrown me off, forsaken me   200

183. Your] *Q1–3, C1–2, S;* You,
H.

---

200. *forsaken me*] Imoinda's remark suggests something of the
fevered portrayal of marital relations in Behn's account of the blacks
of West Africa: "For Wives have a Respect for their Husbands equal
to what any other People pay a Diety; and when a Man finds any
Occasion to quit his Wife, if he love her, she dies by his Hand; if not,
he sells her, or suffers some other to kill her" (Behn, 5: 202). Behn
also delves into the subject of polygamy.

And my misfortunes. That had been a death
Indeed of terror to have trembled at.

OROONOKO.

Forsaken! Thrown thee off!

IMOINDA.

But 'tis a pleasure more than life can give,
That with unconquered passion to the last   205
You struggle still and fain would hold me to you.

OROONOKO.

Ever, ever, and let those stars which are my enemies
Witness against me in the other world,
If I would leave this mansion of my bliss
To be the brightest ruler of their skies.   210

Embracing her.

O! That we could incorporate, be one,
One body, as we have been long one mind.
That blended so, we might together mix,
And losing thus our beings to the world,
Be only found to one another's joys.   215

IMOINDA.

Is this the way to part?

OROONOKO.   Which is the way?

IMOINDA.

The god of love is blind and cannot find it.
But quick, make haste, our enemies have eyes
To find us out and show us the worst way
Of parting; think on them.   220

OROONOKO.

Why dost thou wake me?

IMOINDA.   O! No more of love.
For if I listen to you, I shall quite
Forget my dangers and desire to live.
I can't live yours.   *Takes up the dagger.*

OROONOKO.   There all the stings of death
Are shot into my heart—what shall I do?   225

IMOINDA.

This dagger will instruct you.   *Gives it him.*

OROONOKO.   Ha! This dagger!
Like fate it points me to the horrid deed.

IMOINDA.

    Strike, strike it home and bravely save us both.

    There is no other safety.

OROONOKO.   It must be—

    But first a dying kiss—   *Kisses her.*

                   This last embrace—   230

                        Embracing her.

    And now—

IMOINDA.   I'm ready.

OROONOKO.   O! Where shall I strike?

    Is there a smallest grain of that loved body

    That is not dearer to me than my eyes,

    My bosomed heart, and all the lifeblood there?

    Bid me cut off these limbs, hew off these hands,   235

    Dig out these eyes, though I would keep them last

    To gaze upon thee. But to murder thee!

    The joy and charm of every ravished sense,

    My wife! Forbid it, nature.

IMOINDA.   'Tis your wife

    Who on her knees conjures you. O! In time   240

    Prevent those mischiefs that are falling on us.

    You may be hurried to a shameful death,

    And I too dragged to the vile Governor.

    Then I may cry aloud; when you are gone

    Where shall I find a friend again to save me?   245

OROONOKO.

    It will be so. Thou unexampled virtue!

    Thy resolution has recovered mine.

    And now prepare thee.

IMOINDA.   Thus with open arms

    I welcome you, and death.

He drops his dagger as he looks on her and throws himself
on the ground.

OROONOKO.   I cannot bear it.

    O let me dash against this rock of fate.   250

    Dig up this earth, tear, tear her bowels out

229. safety.] *C2, S*; safety, *Q1–3,*   234. lifeblood] life-blood *C1–2,*
C1, H.   *S*; live blood *Q1–3, H.*

To make a grave deep as the center down
To swallow wide and bury us together!
It wonnot be. O! Then some pitying god
(If there be one a friend to innocence)　　　　　　　255
Find yet a way to lay her beauties down
Gently in death and save me from her blood.

IMOINDA.

O rise! 'Tis more than death to see you thus.
I'll ease your love and do the deed myself—

She takes up the dagger, he rises in haste to take it from her.

OROONOKO.

O! Hold, I charge thee, hold.

IMOINDA.　　　　　　　　　　　Though I must own　　256 260
It would be nobler for us both from you.

OROONOKO.

O! For a whirlwind's wing to hurry us
To yonder cliff which frowns upon the flood
That in embraces locked we might plunge in
And perish thus in one another's arms.　　　[*A shout.*] 265

IMOINDA.

Alas! What shout is that?

OROONOKO.　　　　　　　　I see 'em coming.
They shannot overtake us. This last kiss.
And now farewell.

IMOINDA.　　　　　　　Farewell, farewell forever.

OROONOKO.

I'll turn my face away and do it so.
Now, are you ready?

IMOINDA.　　　　　　　Now. But do not grudge me　270
The pleasure in my death of a last look.
Pray look upon me—now I'm satisfied.

OROONOKO.

So fate must be by this.

Going to stab her he stops short; she lays her hands on his in order to give the blow.

IMOINDA.

Nay then I must assist you.
And since it is the common cause of both,　　　　　275

'Tis just that both should be employed in it.   *Stabs herself.*
Thus, thus 'tis finished, and I bless my fate
That where I lived, I die, in these loved arms.   *Dies.*

OROONOKO.
    She's gone. And now all's at an end with me.
    Soft, lay her down. O, we will part no more.   280
                              Throws himself by her.
    But let me pay the tribute of my grief,
    A few sad tears to thy loved memory,   *Weeps over her.*
    And then I follow—   *A noise again.*
                    But I stay too long.
    The noise comes nearer. Hold, before I go
    There's something would be done. It shall be so.   285
    And then, Imoinda, I'll come all to thee.   *Rises.*

Blanford *and his party enter before the* Governor *and his party,
swords drawn on both sides.*

GOVERNOR.
    You strive in vain to save him; he shall die.
BLANFORD.
    Not while we can defend him with our lives.
GOVERNOR.
    Where is he?
OROONOKO.   Here's the wretch whom you would have.
    Put up your swords and let civil broils   290
    Engage you in the cursed cause of one
    Who cannot live and now entreats to die.
    This object will convince you.   *They gather about the body.*
BLANFORD.   'Tis his wife!
    Alas! There was no other remedy.
GOVERNOR.
    Who did the bloody deed?
OROOONKO.   The deed was mine.   295
    Bloody I know it is and I expect
    Your laws should tell me so. Thus self-condemned,
    I do resign myself into your hands,

---

290. *Put up your swords*] Like so much in this final scene an echo
of Shakespeare's *Othello* (I.ii.59).

The hands of justice—but I hold the sword
For you—and for myself.   300

Stabs the Governor *and himself, then throws himself by Imoinda's
body.*

STANMORE.
He has killed the Governor and stabbed himself.
OROONOKO.
'Tis as it should be now. I have sent his ghost
To be a witness of that happiness
In the next world which he denied us here.   *Dies.*
BLANFORD.
I hope there is a place of happiness   305
In the next world for such exalted virtue.
Pagan or unbeliever, yet he lived
To all he knew; and if he went astray,
There's mercy still above to set him right.
But Christians guided by the heavenly ray   310
Have no excuse if we mistake our way.

FINIS

---

301. *He . . . himself.*] Although Behn's Oroonoko wants to murder
Byam, he never has the opportunity. His death, as well as the murder
of Imoinda, is in keeping with the heroic barbarism of Behn's novella.
Southerne here has in mind Othello's stabbing of Iago and then his
own suicide.

EPILOGUE

Written by Mr. Congreve,
and spoken by Mrs. Verbruggen [as Charlotte].

You see, we try all shapes and shifts and arts
To tempt your favors and regain your hearts.
We weep and laugh, join mirth and grief together,
Like rain and sunshine mixed in April weather.
Your different tastes divide our poet's cares: 5
One foot the sock, t'other the buskin wears.
Thus, while he strives to please, he's forced to do't,
Like Volscius, hip-hop, in a single boot.
Critics, he knows, for this may damn his books,
But he makes feasts for friends and not for cooks.   10
Though errant-knights of late no favor find,
Sure you will be to ladies-errant kind.
To follow fame knights-errant make profession;

Epilogue] *follows* Prologue Q2;
*om. Q3 (CLC). For abbreviations
used here, see Introduction, fn. 1.*
0.3. and . . . Verbruggen] *Q1–*

2, Q3 *(F)*, C1–2, S; *om. Q3 (CLC)*,
H.
6. buskin] Q2, C2; buskins Q1,
Q3 *(F)*, H, C1, S; *om. Q3 (CLC)*.

0.2. *Congreve*] Southerne and William Congreve were friends. Southerne aided Congreve with his first play, *The Old Bachelor* (1693), and they travelled to Ireland together in 1696 to receive Masters of Arts degrees from Trinity College, Dublin.

8. *Volscius*] Prince Volscius in the Duke of Buckingham's burlesque of heroic drama, *The Rehearsal* (III.v.71–94), compares his conflict between love and honor to his state of having one boot on and one still off. He illustrates the point by hopping off the stage in this condition. *The Rehearsal*, which was first staged in 1671, retained its popularity throughout the century.

10. *feasts . . . cooks*] Martial *Epigrams*, 9. 81: "Reader and hearer approve of my works, Aulus, but a certain poet says they are not polished. I don't care much, for I should prefer the courses of my dinner to please guests rather than cooks" (trans. Walter C. A. Ker, Loeb Library, 2: 133).

11. *errant-knights*] This is a reference to the third part of Durfey's *Don Quixote*, produced about the same time as *Oroonoko* in November 1695. The first two parts had been well received, and Durfey blamed the performers of the songs and dances for the ill success of the third part.

We damsels fly to save our reputation:
So they, their valor show; we, our discretion.   15
To lands of monsters and fierce beasts they go,
We to those islands where rich husbands grow.
Though they're no monsters, we may make 'em so.
If they're of English growth, they'll bear't with patience,
But save us from a spouse of Oroonoko's nations!   20
Then bless your stars, you happy London wives,
Who love at large, each day, yet keep your lives.
Nor envy poor Imoinda's doting blindness,
Who thought her husband killed her out of kindness.
Death with a husband ne'er had shown such charms,   25
Had she once died within a lover's arms.
Her error was from ignorance proceeding.
Poor soul! She wanted some of our town breeding.
Forgive this Indian's fondness of her spouse;
Their law no Christian liberty allows.   30
Alas! They make a conscience of their vows!
If virtue in a heathen be a fault,
Then damn the heathen school where she was taught.
She might have learned to cuckold, jilt, and sham
Had Covent Garden been in Surinam.   35

FINIS

---

17. *islands*] Given the shortage of men willing to marry in England, many women sought husbands in the West Indies, as Charlotte and Lucy do in Surinam.

18. *monsters*] a reference to the usual image of that horned monster, the cuckold.

26. *died*] a common sexual pun still current in the Restoration.

29. *Indian's*] i.e., Imoinda's. Congreve may be thinking of Behn's description of the fidelity of African wives, or he may associate her with the Indian wives who refused to live after their husband's death.

30. *Christian liberty*] a commonplace irony in the Restoration suggesting that female libertinism might find some justification in Christian doctrine. See, for example, Alexander Radcliffe's lines:

> I gave him all Christian Liberty,
> I let him sometimes lig [lie] by me,
> I let him feel my Duchesses Knee

("To a Late Scotch Tune," *The Ramble* [London, 1682], p. 40).

35. *Covent Garden*] the resort of prostitutes and men of gallantry.

Appendix A

Additional Music for *Oroonoko*

Only two songs are included in the text of *Oroonoko*: "A lass there lives upon the green" and "Bright Cynthia's pow'r divinely great" (II.iii.80–94 and 95–110). There is the possibility, however, that a third song was planned for or actually performed in some productions.

Henry Playford, one of the original publishers of *Oroonoko*, was also one of the most important music publishers of the Restoration. The Fourth Book of his *Deliciae Musicae* (1696) includes the caption "The three following Songs, in the Play call'd *Oroonoko*." The first two songs are those in the text. They are immediately followed (page 7) by "A Dialogue Sung in *Oroonoko*, by the Boy and Girl. Sett by Mr. *Henry Purcell*," which begins "Celemene, pray tell me," with music typical of Purcell in his late Italianate period and words by Thomas Durfey.

It was apparently customary for at least three songs to be sung in a dramatic performance in the fall of 1695. Most of the songs of Rich's Company found their way into *Deliciae Musicae* or into John Simpson's *Thesaurus Musicus,* and in a great many of them Durfey and Purcell had a hand. There would seem to be a good reason then for accepting "Celemene" as belonging to *Oroonoko* either in actuality or intention. There is, however, in the British Museum an engraved single sheet, ca. 1700, done by "Tho. Cross" (whom Playford later decried for "Scandalous Abuse of Musick by selling single Songs at a Penny a piece"),[1] which attributes "Celemene" to John Dryden's *Conquest of Granada, Part II. Conquest II* was first performed in December 1670, and one of its many editions was published in 1696; but none of the editions, that of 1696 or those earlier or later, includes this song.

The confusion surrounding the placement of the song may have had to do with the death of Purcell on 21 November 1695, the month of the initial performance of *Oroonoko.* Then there is the possible absence of Letitia Cross, the child prodigy whom

Purcell favored and for whom he probably wrote this piece. In September and October of 1695 Miss Cross had specific roles in new productions at Drury Lane. In November her name is missing from the cast list of *Oroonoko*, and she is mentioned only in the text of the published play at II.iii.79.6, where the stage directions indicate that a song is to be "sung by the Boy to Miss Cross." *The London Stage* does not include her name in any roster for December. But in January, February, and March of 1696 she is again assigned either a small part or the epilogue.

We might speculate that without Miss Cross to sing "Celemene" at the premiere the song somehow became dissociated from the original play text. Whatever the reason for the exclusion of "Celemene" from all the editions of *Oroonoko*, Purcell's air with Durfey's teasing words can be enjoyed for its own sake.

A Dialogue Sung in *Oroonoko* by the Boy and Girl
Set by Mr. Henry Purcell

He: Celemene, pray tell me; pray tell me, Celemene,
When those pretty eyes I see
Why my heart beats in my breast?
Why it will not let me rest?
Why this trembling too all o'er,
Pains I never felt before?
And when thus I touch your hand
Why I wish I was a man?

She: How should I know more than you,
Yet would be a woman, too?
When you wash yourself and play
I methinks could look all day.
Nay, just now am pleased so well,
Should you kiss me I won't tell.
No, no, I won't tell;
Should you kiss me I won't tell.

He: Though I could do that all day
And desire no better play,
Sure in love there's something more
Which makes Mama so big before.

She: Once by chance I heard it named;
Don't ask what, for I'm ashamed.

> Stay but till you're past fifteen;
> Then you'll know what 'tis I mean.

He: However, lose not present bliss,
But now we're alone let's kiss.

She: My breasts do so heave;

He: my heart does so pant,

He ⎱
She ⎰: There's something more we want.

1. Quoted by Cyrus Lawrence Day and Eleanore Boswell Murrie, "English Song-Books, 1651–1702, and their Publishers," *The Library*, 4th Series, Vol. XVI, no. 4 (March 1936), p. 389n.

Appendix B

Chronology

Approximate dates are indicated by *. Dates for plays are those on which they were first made public, either on stage or in print.

Political and Literary Events	*Life and Major Works of Southerne*

1631
Death of Donne.
John Dryden born.
1633
Samuel Pepys born.
1635
Sir George Etherege born.*
1640
Aphra Behn born.*
1641
William Wycherley born.*
1642
First Civil War began (ended 1646).
Theaters closed by Parliament.
Thomas Shadwell born.*
1648
Second Civil War.
Nathaniel Lee born.*
1649
Execution of Charles I.
1650
Jeremy Collier born.
1651
Hobbes' *Leviathan* published.
1652
First Dutch War began (ended

1654).
Thomas Otway born.

1656
D'Avenant's *THE SIEGE OF RHODES* performed at Rutland House.

1657
John Dennis born.

1658
Death of Oliver Cromwell.
D'Avenant's *THE CRUELTY OF THE SPANIARDS IN PERU* performed at the Cockpit.

1659

Born at Oxmantown near Dublin 12 February.

1660
Restoration of Charles II.
Theatrical patents granted to Thomas Killigrew and Sir William D'Avenant, authorizing them to form, respectively, the King's and the Duke of York's Companies.
Pepys began his diary.

1661
Cowley's *THE CUTTER OF COLEMAN STREET*.
D'Avenant's *THE SIEGE OF RHODES* (expanded to two parts).

1662
Charter granted to the Royal Society.

1663
Dryden's *THE WILD GALLANT*.
Tuke's *THE ADVENTURES OF FIVE HOURS*.

1664
Sir John Vanbrugh born.
Dryden's *THE RIVAL LADIES*.
Dryden and Howard's *THE IN-*

DIAN QUEEN.
Etherege's *THE COMICAL RE-VENGE.*

1665
Second Dutch War began (ended 1667).
Great Plague.
Dryden's *THE INDIAN EM-PEROR.*
Orrery's *MUSTAPHA.*

1666
Fire of London.
Death of James Shirley.

1667
Jonathan Swift born.
Milton's *Paradise Lost* published.
Sprat's *The History of the Royal Society* published.
Dryden's *SECRET LOVE.*

1668
Death of D'Avenant.
Dryden made Poet Laureate.
Dryden's *An Essay of Dramatic Poesy* published.
Shadwell's *THE SULLEN LOV-ERS.*
Etherege's *SHE WOULD IF SHE COULD.*

1669
Pepys terminated his diary.
Susanna Centlivre born.

1670
William Congreve born.
Dryden's *THE CONQUEST OF GRANADA,* Part I.

1671
Dorset Garden Theatre (Duke's Company) opened.
Colley Cibber born.
Milton's *Paradise Regained* and *Samson Agonistes* published.

Dryden's *THE CONQUEST OF GRANADA*, Part II.
Dryden's *MARRIAGE A LA MODE*.
THE REHEARSAL, by the Duke of Buckingham and others.
Wycherley's *LOVE IN A WOOD*.

1672
Third Dutch War began (ended 1674).
Joseph Addison born.
Richard Steele born.

1674
New Drury Lane Theatre (King's Company) opened.
Death of Milton.
Nicholas Rowe born.
Thomas Rymer's *Reflections on Aristotle's Treatise of Poesy* (translation of Rapin) published.

1675
Dryden's *AURENG-ZEBE*.
Wycherley's *THE COUNTRY WIFE*.*

1676
Etherege's *THE MAN OF MODE*.
Otway's *DON CARLOS*.
Shadwell's *THE VIRTUOSO*.
Wycherley's *THE PLAIN DEAL-ER*.

Admitted as pensioner to Trinity College 30 March.

1677
Aphra Behn's *THE ROVER*.
Dryden's *ALL FOR LOVE*.
Lee's *THE RIVAL QUEENS*.
Rymer's *Tragedies of the Last Age Considered* published.

1678
Popish Plot.
George Farquhar born.
Bunyan's *Pilgrim's Progress* (Part I) published.

1679

Exclusion Bill introduced.
Death of Thomas Hobbes.
Death of Roger Boyle, Earl of Orrery.
Charles Johnson born.

1680

Death of Samuel Butler.
Death of John Wilmot, Earl of Rochester.
Dryden's *THE SPANISH FRIAR*.
Lee's *LUCIUS JUNIUS BRUTUS*.
Otway's *THE ORPHAN*.

Arrived in London from Dublin. Admitted to Middle Temple 15 July.

1681

Charles II dissolved Parliament at Oxford.
Dryden's *Absalom and Achitophel* published.
Tate's adaptation of *KING LEAR*.

1682

The King's and the Duke of York's Companies merged into the United Company.
Dryden's *The Medal, MacFlecknoe*, and *Religio Laici* published.
Otway's *VENICE PRESERVED*.

THE LOYAL BROTHER, OR THE PERSIAN PRINCE (Drury Lane, February), Prologue and Epilogue written by Dryden. Tachmas, the hero, represented the future James II; the play was intended as a compliment to him.

1683

Rye House Plot.
Death of Thomas Killigrew.
Crowne's *CITY POLITIQUES*.

1684

THE DISAPPOINTMENT, OR THE MOTHER IN FASHION (Drury Lane, April), Prologue by Dryden, with Betterton as Alphonso.

1685

Death of Charles II; accession of James II.
Revocation of the Edict of

THE DISAPPOINTMENT performed for the King and Queen on 27 January.

Nantes.

The Duke of Monmouth's Rebellion.

Death of Otway.

John Gay born.

Crowne's *SIR COURTLY NICE.*

Dryden's *ALBION AND ALBANIUS.*

1686

1687

Death of the Duke of Buckingham.

Dryden's *The Hind and the Panther* published.

Newton's *Principia* published.

1688

The Revolution.

Alexander Pope born.

Shadwell's *THE SQUIRE OF ALSATIA.*

1689

The War of the League of Augsburg began (ended 1697).

Toleration Act.

Death of Aphra Behn.

Shadwell made Poet Laureate.

Dryden's *DON SEBASTIAN.*

Shadwell's *BURY FAIR.*

1690

Battle of the Boyne.

Locke's *Two Treatises of Government* and *An Essay Concerning Human Understanding* published.

1691

Death of Etherege.*

Langbaine's *An Account of the English Dramatic Poets* published.

1692

Death of Lee.

Southerne granted a commission as ensign on 19 June in the Princess Anne's Regiment of Foot by James Fitz-James, later Duke of Berwick, the natural son of James II.

Raised to rank of lieutenant on 1 June.

Work begun on *THE SPARTAN DAME.*

Forced to leave his regiment as a consequence of the Revolution.

SIR ANTHONY LOVE, OR THE RAMBLING LADY (Drury Lane, October).

"The Charming Bride," a broadside, published.

THE WIVES EXCUSE, OR CUCKOLDS MAKE THEMSELVES (Drury Lane, December).

Death of Shadwell.
Tate made Poet Laureate.

1693

George Lillo born.*
Rymer's *A Short View on Tragedy* published.
Congreve's *THE OLD BACHE-LOR*.

THE MAID'S LAST PRAYER, OR ANY RATHER THAN FALL (Drury Lane, January).
Southerne arranged with Thomas D'Avenant for the first performance of Congreve's *OLD BACHE-LOR*.
Dryden entrusted Southerne with the revision and completion of his tragedy *Cleomenes*.

1694

Death of Queen Mary.

THE FATAL MARRIAGE, OR THE INNOCENT ADULTERY (Drury Lane, February) with Elizabeth Barry, adapted from Aphra Behn's *The Nun, or the Fair Vow-breaker*.

1695

Group of actors led by Thomas Betterton left Drury Lane and established a new company at Lincoln's Inn Fields.
Congreve's *LOVE FOR LOVE*.

OROONOKO (Drury Lane, November) with Verbruggen as Oroonoko.

1696

Cibber's *LOVE'S LAST SHIFT*.
Vanbrugh's *THE RELAPSE*.

Awarded M.A. degree by Trinity College.
Cibber's *Love's Last Shift* accepted for performance at Drury Lane in January upon Southerne's recommendation.
Southerne sponsored Richard Norton's *Pausanius, The Betrayer of His Country* (Drury Lane, 3 April).

1697

Treaty of Ryswick ended the War of the League of Augsburg.
Charles Macklin born.
Congreve's *THE MOURNING BRIDE*.

Vanbrugh's *THE PROVOKED WIFE.*

1698

Collier controversy started with the publication of *A Short View of the Immorality and Profaneness of the English Stage.*

1699.

Farquhar's *THE CONSTANT COUPLE.*

1700

Death of Dryden.
Blackmore's *Satire against Wit* published.
Congreve's *THE WAY OF THE WORLD.*

THE FATE OF CAPUA (Lincoln's Inn Fields, April).

1701

Act of Settlement.
War of the Spanish Succession began (ended 1713).
Death of James II.
Rowe's *TAMERLANE.*
Steele's *THE FUNERAL.*

1702

Death of William III; accession of Anne.
The Daily Courant began publication.
Cibber's *SHE WOULD AND SHE WOULD NOT.*

A Comparison between the Two Stages, which includes praise of Southerne, published.

1703

Death of Samuel Pepys.
Rowe's *THE FAIR PENITENT.*

Southerne believed to have left the stage. An anonymous satirical poem, "Religio Poetae: or, A Satyr on the Poets," refers to Southerne's improved financial circumstances since his marriage.

1704

Capture of Gibraltar; Battle of Blenheim.
Defoe's *The Review* began publication (1704–1713).

Advised John Dennis on *Liberty Asserted.*

Swift's *A Tale of a Tub* and *The Battle of the Books* published.

Cibber's *THE CARELESS HUS-BAND*.

1705

Haymarket Theatre opened.

Steele's *THE TENDER HUS-BAND*.

1706

Battle of Ramillies.

Farquhar's *THE RECRUITING OFFICER*.

1707

Union of Scotland and England.

Death of Farquhar.

Henry Fielding born.

Farquhar's *THE BEAUX' STRATAGEM*.

1708

Downe's *Roscius Anglicanus* published.

1709

Samuel Johnson born.

Rowe's edition of Shakespeare published.

The Tatler began publication (1709–1711).

Centlivre's *THE BUSY BODY*.

1711

Shaftesbury's *Characteristics* published.

The Spectator began publication (1711–1712).

Pope's *An Essay on Criticism* published.

1713

Treaty of Utrecht ended the War of the Spanish Succession.

Addison's *CATO*.

1714

Death of Anne; accession of George I.

Steele became Governor of Drury Lane.
John Rich assumed management of Lincoln's Inn Fields.
Centlivre's *THE WONDER: A WOMAN KEEPS A SECRET*.
Rowe's *JANE SHORE*.

1715
Jacobite Rebellion.
Death of Tate.
Rowe made Poet Laureate.
Death of Wycherley.

1716
Addison's *THE DRUMMER*.

1717
David Garrick born.
Cibber's *THE NON-JUROR*.
Gay, Pope, and Arbuthnot's *THREE HOURS AFTER MARRIAGE*.

1718
Death of Rowe.
Centlivre's *A BOLD STROKE FOR A WIFE*.

1719
Death of Addison.
Defoe's *Robinson Crusoe* published.
Young's *BUSIRIS, KING OF EGYPT*.

THE SPARTAN DAME (Drury Lane, 11 December).

1720
South Sea Bubble.
Samuel Foote born.
Steele suspended from the Governorship of Drury Lane (restored 1721).
Little Theatre in the Haymarket opened. Steele's *The Theatre* (periodical) published.
Hughes' *THE SIEGE OF DAMASCUS*.

1721
Walpole became first Minister.

1722
Steele's *THE CONSCIOUS LOVERS*.

1723
Death of Susanna Centlivre.
Death of D'Urfey.

1725
Pope's edition of Shakespeare published.

1726
Death of Jeremy Collier.
Death of Vanbrugh.
Law's *Unlawfulness of Stage Entertainments* published
Swift's *Gulliver's Travels* published.

MONEY THE MISTRESS (Lincoln's Inn Fields, February) opened and immediately failed.

1727
Death of George I; accession of George II.
Death of Sir Isaac Newton.
Arthur Murphy born.

1728
Pope's *The Dunciad* (first version) published.
Cibber's *THE PROVOKED HUSBAND* (expansion of Vanbrugh's fragment *A JOURNEY TO LONDON*).
Gay's *THE BEGGAR'S OPERA*.

1729
Goodman's Fields Theatre opened.
Death of Congreve.
Death of Steele.
Edmund Burke born.

1730
Cibber made Poet Laureate.
Oliver Goldsmith born.
Thomson's *The Seasons* published.
Fielding's *THE AUTHOR'S FARCE*.

Fielding's *TOM THUMB* (revised
as *THE TRAGEDY OF TRAGE-
DIES*, 1731).

1731
Death of Defoe.
Fielding's *THE GRUB-STREET
OPERA*.
Lillo's *THE LONDON MER-
CHANT*.

1732
Covent Garden Theatre opened.
Death of Gay.
George Colman the elder born.
Fielding's *THE COVENT GAR-
DEN TRAGEDY*.
Fielding's *THE MODERN HUS-
BAND*.
Charles Johnson's *CAELIA*.

1733
Pope's *An Essay on Man* (Epistles
I–III) published (Epistle IV, 1734).

1734
Death of Dennis.
The Prompter began publication
(1734–1736).
Theobald's edition of Shakespeare
published.
Fielding's *DON QUIXOTE IN
ENGLAND*.

1736
Fielding led the "Great Mogul's
Company of Comedians" at the
Little Theatre in the Haymarket
(1736–1737).
Fielding's *PASQUIN*.
Lillo's *FATAL CURIOSITY*.

Began his ten-year stay with Mr.
Whyte in Tothill Street in Westminster. Known for his faithful
attendance of worship at Westminster Abbey. Wrote "Memoirs
relating to Mr. Congreve."

1737
The Stage Licensing Act.
Dodsley's *THE KING AND THE
MILLER OF MANSFIELD*.
Fielding's *THE HISTORICAL
REGISTER FOR 1736*.

Pope praised Southerne as a
writer skilled in expressing "the
passions" in his "Imitations of
Horace" (Epistle 2.1.86).

1738

Johnson's *London* published.
Pope's *One Thousand Seven Hundred and Thirty-Eight* published.
Thomson's *AGAMEMNON*.

1739

War with Spain began.
Death of Lillo.
Hugh Kelly born.
Fielding's *The Champion* began publication (1739–41).
Johnson's *Complete Vindication of Licensers of the Stage,* an ironical criticism of the Licensing Act, published after Brooke's *GUSTAVUS VASA* was denied a license.

1740

War of the Austrian Succession began (ended 1748).
James Boswell born.
Cibber's *Apology for His Life* published.
Richardson's *Pamela* published.
Garrick's *LETHE*.
Thomson and Mallet's *ALFRED*.

1741

Edmund Malone born.
Garrick began acting.
Fielding's *Shamela* published.
Garrick's *THE LYING VALET*.

1742

Walpole resigned his offices.
Cibber's *Letters to Mr. Pope* published.
Fielding's *Joseph Andrews* published.
Pope's *New Dunciad* (Book IV of *The Dunciad*) published.
Young's *The Complaint,* or *Night Thoughts* published (additional parts published each year until 1745).

Pope addressed a further congratulatory verse, "*Tom Southerne*'s Birth-day Dinner at LD. *Orrey*'s," to Southerne on the occasion of his eighty-third birthday. The verse printed in *Gentleman's Magazine* (February).

1743
Death of Henry Carey.
Fielding's *Miscellanies* published.
1744
Death of Pope.
Death of Theobald.
Dodsley's *A Select Collection of Old Plays* published.
Johnson's *Life of Mr. Richard Savage* published.
1745
Jacobite Rebellion.
Death of Swift.
Thomas Holcroft born.
Johnson's *Observations on Macbeth* published.
Thomson's *TANCRED AND SIGISMUNDA*.
1746
Collins's *Odes* published.

Died on Monday, 26 May, at Smith Street in Westminster. Buried in St. Margaret's Church, Westminster, 29 May.
Agnes Southerne, daughter, married 29 November.